C000047243

ANITA MENDIRATTA

THE CALL TO
LEADERSHIP

UNLOCKING THE LEADER WITHIN IN TIMES OF CRISIS

First published in Great Britain in 2023 by

Anita Mendiratta, in partnership with whitefox publishing

www.wearewhitefox.com

www.thecalltoleadership.com

Hardback ISBN 978-1-915635-68-6

eBook ISBN 978-1-915635-69-3

Audiobook ISBN 978-1-915635-70-9

Cover and interior design by Hybert Design

Project management by whitefox

Printed and bound by CPI Group (UK) Ltd, Croydon CR0 4YY

To salute those who carried us through,
and to honour those who we now carry in memory.

CONTENTS

FOREWORD

Tourism has a unique power to bring people together. It is a vibrant and dynamic sector, driving economic growth, generating employment, and fostering cross-cultural understanding. But at its heart are people and human connections. That is why tourism has always been a beacon of hope in times of uncertainty. It is also how I came to know Anita, and our shared belief in the transformative power of tourism serves as the foundation of our working and personal relationship.

Both of us were witness to the devastation caused to global tourism by the pandemic. We also knew to look beyond the numbers. We recognised that behind each statistic around falling arrivals, there was a story: a job lost or a business forced to close. As the Secretary-General of the World Tourism Organization (UNWTO) of the United Nations, I saw first-hand the tremendous challenges faced by leaders in the tourism sector and beyond in the midst of the crisis. It was a time of great uncertainty and apprehension, and a time when we needed calm, measured voices more than ever. Anita stood out. When others panicked, she remained clear-headed.

Anita played a key role in advising leaders through some of the darkest days of the crisis. Above all, her deep expertise and experience contributed to uniting them behind a focused plan of action that was crucial as UNWTO worked to lead our sector's response and recovery. Now her book, *The Call to Leadership*, brings together the stories and lessons learned from many of these exceptional individuals.

While the biggest crisis in the history of our sector looms large, the stories also focus on the personal experiences of all of those leaders, myself included. They speak of doubts, but also optimism and hope. And in this way these stories offer a valuable insight into not only what decisions were taken, but why they were taken, what that means for the future of the sector we are all so fortunate to work in, and how we can make these lessons a part of tourism education, one of UNWTO's key priorities for the years ahead.

This is especially relevant now, as we enter a new chapter. The reopening of borders and the revitalisation of global travel brings us reason to be hopeful and look ahead to a bright and positive future. It is one that brings new challenges as well as new opportunities. We have good reason to hope. To make the most of it, we will need to rethink how we communicate, and how the world outside our sector sees – and appreciates – tourism. UNWTO is fully embracing this chance. Though our mission remains the same, our identity is being reimagined for a new era, determined to always put people first as we place tourism high on the agenda of governments and international organisations everywhere.

I extend my deepest appreciation to Anita for ensuring that lessons learned are not lost. I have every confidence that this book will inspire and empower leaders around the world to answer their call to leadership, while at the same time inspiring global youth, enabling a stronger and more resilient future not just for tourism but for humanity.

ZURAB POLOLIKASHVILI
SECRETARY-GENERAL, UNITED NATIONS WORLD TOURISM ORGANIZATION (UNWTO)

PREFACE

It's hard.

It's hard to write about a time that everyone wants to forget.

A time when, whether around the corner or across the world, we were all kept apart. Home visiting, holiday travelling, handshakes, hugging – it all stopped.

Celebrations for big birthdays, blessings of new-born babies, honouring of graduates, meetings between colleagues and companies, forums of global industries, first dances of newlyweds and final goodbyes to those adored, had to be either left out or lived out online.

It's hard to write about a chapter in our lives that so painfully impacted the story of our lives. A time when people lost so much.

They lost loved ones,

their livelihoods,

their legacy,

their homes and

their hope.

A time when fear for our health was front and centre,

when frontliners worked around the clock for us,

with little rest, little reward and little thanks.

It's hard to return to a time when the world is understandably trying to move as far away from it as possible.

It's hard to focus on a time that can feel to have been a blur, so lacking in distinct detail, understanding of what was happening, and confidence that we were all going to make it through.

It's hard to reflect on a time when so many were so deeply challenged personally, professionally, economically, morally, spiritually, operationally, individually and collectively.

It's hard.

Time moves on. The world has moved on. People have started to forget. People have chosen to forget.

And yet it's even harder to ignore the humanitarian crisis we all lived through, casually walking away without taking the lessons with us. It's hard to bury in the past what we know will provide critical wisdom for our future. Hence, *The Call to Leadership*.

This book is a response to a calling that I have felt deeply and heard loudly since the early days of a global pandemic that stopped, shook and reshaped our world. And for a period of time galvanised our world. Mother Nature had to have known what she was doing. She had to have a reason for grounding us all and, in doing so, forcing us all to look closely at our lives, at our choices, at our impact – at ourselves. Importantly, she forced us to look at our relationships with, and responsibility towards, others – family, friends, colleagues, neighbours and even strangers.

She must have had a reason.

The Call to Leadership brings together a world of leaders from government, business and academia, people I am privileged to know personally as colleagues, as clients, as friends. They are leaders who gave me their trust, making their inner voices audible to allow me access into their minds and hearts as they recalled facing the global pandemic and some of the hardest, most defining times in their lives, that they now know have shaped who they are as leaders today. Through their recollections and through their reflections they show why it is impossible for some leaders to look away when a crisis occurs. They could not *not* step forward.

In that same spirit, I could not *not* write this book. I could not let days, months and years pass without pausing to honour what we have all lived through, to celebrate the ability to persevere and overcome, and to salute those who guided us through, especially the leaders who heard their calling. The brave, bold actions they took in this time – actions that shifted the word 'leader' from a noun to a verb – must be captured and learned from. Their leadership decisions and actions offer us examples of wisdom, insight and intelligence. They also show us what it means to be wired to lead, and how it feels to hear your calling. In so doing they inspire us to recognise and embrace our calling, so that when each of us hears it, we only need to answer one question: Do I have the courage to follow it?

On hearing the calling to create this book the answer was clear: Yes, because 'no' was not an option.

CHAPTER 1

AND THEN A LIGHTHOUSE APPEARED:
THE PRESENCE OF LEADERSHIP IN THE
DARKEST OF TIMES

Hope is not a strategy.

PUNEET CHHATWAL, CEO AND MANAGING DIRECTOR,
INDIAN HOTELS COMPANY LIMITED (IHCL)

The call to leadership. What exactly is it? How does it happen? When? For whom? And importantly, how do you hear it?

A 'calling' is something you may never have actually 'heard' before, not in a literal, heard-out-loud sense. This is not about a defined role, mandate, job description, or set of specific Key Performance Indicators (KPIs). This goes beyond technical description and requires preparation. This is much more personal, almost visceral. It is about a feeling, a feeling that carries within it a whisper calling you to attention, forcing you to recognise that a defining moment of decision-making and action in your life is happening.

It has happened to us all. At some point in time, in some situation when something completely unexpected happened that immediately grabbed our attention and forced us to focus on a crisis right in front of us, we heard a calling. It activated a sense of purpose deep within us. It gave us the strength and courage to step forward even when feeling uncertain. It enabled our inner voice to whisper with absolute certainty 'I hear you'.

These moments in our lives are few, and yet they have the power to shape how we lead our lives. They influence the big decisions we make for ourselves. They set our wiring.

For some, these moments set them on a path of leadership. They come to define who they are for the rest of their lives – people who recognise that they are wired to lead when called upon. We have all recently lived through a time that held within it such a moment, revealing to us such leaders.

Do you remember Q1 2020? No doubt for you, just like myself, it still feels as if it was just yesterday. The roaring 2020s had begun. New hope, new energy, new boldness of all that was going to be bigger, better, bolder. Markets were strong. Aspirations for a new era were even stronger. What could possibly go wrong?

But then, within a matter of weeks, something did not feel right. I, like you, could not see it, nor could we fully understand it, but in our hearts, we knew. Our world was starting to change irreversibly. From East to West, alarms were starting to sound. A previously unknown, rapidly transmissible, increasingly life-threatening virus was starting to spread from Asia to Europe: COVID-19.

By the end of Q1, borders and skies across the globe were shutting. Travel was grounded. Trade was blocked. Markets were collapsing. From Beijing to Bangkok, Bangalore to Beirut, Berlin to Budapest and Barcelona, and everywhere in the world in between, schools were closing, businesses were shuttering, livelihoods were being broken and lives were lost. The roaring 2020s had come with a bite beyond comprehension, and as it would soon be made clear, beyond fiction.

In a vacuum of knowledge and understanding, we found that all of us, as leaders, practitioners, travellers and people, were forced to make massive adjustments to our lifestyles as a way of containing any risk of the virus spreading through our wider community. The radius of our lives was rapidly constricted to 'bubbles' – small, carefully defined circles of people with whom our interactions were limited. Life became about bubbles – family bubbles, work bubbles, social bubbles . . . safety bubbles.

The threat was invisible and challenged everyone's capability to face the unknown. It made us focus on safety – physical, emotional and financial – like never before, dealing with fear, finding hope, and finding a way through.

While the 1918 pandemic had offered some understanding of the risks and consequences of a virus threatening worldwide safety and stability, the current leadership generation lacked those who knew how to lead through a threat of this size, scale and speed. Knowledge was academic – no one had active experience of a worldwide pandemic.

The virus had characteristics that none of us ever expected. It was completely democratic – everyone, everywhere, was at risk. It did not care about borders, religion, earnings, principles or politics. Frighteningly, there was no way of knowing how it was going to unfold, how this story was going to end. Or when.

We were all a living case study. We were forced to write a new chapter in the history of the world, one of intense challenge, change and sometimes even chance. This situation meant everyone was forced to find a way to get through, to find a source of guidance, of confidence, of hope. We searched for anything, anyone, anywhere to help us make sense of the questions we were facing, before we could even begin to find answers. Technology replaced touch. Fear replaced freedom. Standing still replaced everything we once experienced beyond our doors and shores.

Stay home, stay safe. Stay strong. Keep your hands clean. Only 'essential workers' were permitted to move around for purposes of work, for purposes of our protection.

Despite severe restrictions on the lives of the public, in our industry, in governments and in our communities, some individuals were able to step forward with courage and a calmness that became a compass for us to follow, including:

- medical personnel
- COVID-19 response volunteers
- food and medical retail providers, stockists, clerks
- drivers delivering medicines, food, anything actually
- transport-system network providers
- postal-service workers
- faith leaders and so many more who so practically and meaningfully redefined the word 'essential'

These people cared for us and our loved ones. They carried us through the loss of what were once simple luxuries, from loving hugs of 'hello', to grieving tears of 'goodbye' and cries of 'I'm scared'.

Across government departments and businesses, these heroes emerged. Quietly, carefully, almost intuitively, they pushed past the paralysis of their own fear. They heard the call of duty, they faced fear and they stepped forward. They demonstrated, often ever so subtly, that at times of crisis, some people immediately run towards the fire while others run away. We all remember them well; we remember observing their bravery, even if they thought no one was watching. But that was then. What does this have to do with now?

THE POWER OF OUR WIRING

The instinctive, immediate response of these individuals who confidently and courageously run towards the fire can only be defined as their 'wiring' – how they respond in the face of a crisis. Their responses are keyholes for understanding the strength that can be unlocked when a challenge occurs. But watching them is not enough. We need to learn from them to understand:

- What went through their minds?
- What went through their hearts?
- How did they determine their first response? And then, what next?
- How did they control the risks to themselves?
- Why were they so determined to leave no one behind?
- Had something in their past wired them to be able to confront the present?

As our world inscribes those times in the history books, it is far too easy to fast forward into our newly shaping world, forgetting what happened and consciously creating a blind spot that allows us to move forward without being haunted by the past. But as I wrote earlier, that would be fundamentally wrong, as we would waste the time that Mother Nature gave us to comprehend the world around us and our role in it. If we don't take the opportunity to heal, grow and define strength from the challenges we faced, we risk losing a valuable chance to prepare for the next time we are challenged.

We need to learn from it.

We need to grow from it.

And, importantly, we need to respect it.

> *It was a time that erased the line between the professional and the personal. It unlocked behaviours that were primal.*

It was a traumatic time – trauma in the truest sense of the word. Everyone responded in different ways, finding different ways to cope with the fear, the confusion, the pressure and the pain. Everyone, alone.

This book offers a unique exploration of the qualities displayed by leaders who stepped forward during the recent global crisis. Through the experiences and honest, open, highly personal reflections of each of the leaders involved, we are able to gain valuable insights and understanding from their perspective. The interviews in this book provide a raw and authentic perspective on leadership during a time of crisis. Analysing these interviews on a common platform uncovered meaningful, insightful themes of leadership to inspire and guide readers.

More specifically, this book utilises a crisis we can all relate to as an example to help us identify key components in recognising, processing and responding to other crises. It takes a very human approach towards simple, yet vital, aspects of crisis response that are at the heart of mobilising us into helpful action, including:

- making sense of the moment – identifying the real problem
- seeking safety – finding one's own sense of calm and control
- quieting the noise – separating out facts from fear and frenzy
- taking action – deciding 'what *now*?' with an eye towards 'what *next*?'
- leading in the dark – working through unknowns
- connecting through honesty – strength in showing weakness
- staying strong – creating an inner circle of support

This book is *not* intended to be a leadership manual, a checklist of actions, a crisis management plan with metrics, or a self-help guide. Rather, it aims to help us all confront times in our lives when we need to unlock the ability within us to face a storm, personal or professional, be it large or small, individual or collective. It aims to help us to face the darkening skies, find a way into the eye of the storm, find hope in 'after', and ultimately, find a sense of confidence, a sense of purpose, and a sense of hope, even through apparently hopeless times.

Importantly, this book seeks to provide insight into how we can recover from one crisis to prepare to face the next. For there will be another crisis.

And another.

And another.

We need to prepare ourselves for whatever crisis is ahead as individuals and as a collective. The crisis may be internal and highly personal – the loss of a relationship, the loss of a loved one, the loss of a job, or the loss of health. It may be external – a terror attack, a natural disaster, an economic collapse, or a pandemic. Whatever the crisis, what is critical is the ability to find the eye of the storm and safely come through.

So, why are we still talking about COVID-19?

Simply this: the global pandemic provides us with a canvas that we can all share. It is an experience that we have all gone through recently together, even if we felt very alone. It is fresh in our memories. It is something we can all tap into as a shared memory with high credibility because it has been so recent. *The Call to Leadership* is about understanding, through a shared point of reference, the wiring that leaders had that enabled them to respond to the crisis when they heard their calling.

Under no circumstances is this book a desire to rip off the Band-Aid. You and I know all too well that many people the world over are anxious to put that time behind them, consciously forgetting all that was endured when the world not only slowed but stopped, when life felt almost fictional. They would rather fast-forward into the future.

So why take people back to experience the hurt once more? Why, when now is the time for healing? That is exactly why this shared canvas is used: for healing, for strength, for confidence.

Healing comes from building strength and confidence. Strength and confidence that are unlocked through understanding, that turns clarity into insight,

insight into wisdom,

wisdom into confidence,

confidence into inner strength,

inner strength into peace of mind when facing the future, whatever the future may bring.

This chapter of history provides us with not only a common context and understanding, but also a basis for human connection. This connection brings us together as a community, so that we can learn from one another, whoever and wherever we are in the world, whatever keeps us busy each day. It helped us all come through the pandemic smarter, stronger and more confident. This human connection also enables us to believe in the presence of a rainbow after the rain.

The Call to Leadership consciously focuses on the travel and tourism sector and leaders from government, business, media, academia and others because they offer a unique and diverse perspective on leadership during this uniquely challenging period in our lifetime. And yet this book is not intended to be a study of COVID-19, specific leaders, travelling, or even tourism. This book's aim is to be an opportunity to look back at this time for what it truly was – a living case study.

Because within that case study are lessons on the ability of a crisis to unlock in some people a 'superpower', especially when these people recognised how their wiring not only worked, but became a tool, to get them and others through safely.

This book purposefully connects with twenty highly qualified, respected, appreciated high-level leaders that we often saw daily during the pandemic, each bravely stepping forward to help us find the eye in the storm, and then through it to the safer other side. From Asia and Africa to the Americas, the Middle East and Europe, they are leaders in sectors critical to global growth, development and stability, including government, big business, media, academia, aviation, hotel companies and emergency response. They are people who, in 'business as usual' times, traditionally preferred to just get on with their mandates in their respective spheres of operation and influence.

And yet, when a crisis called, these leaders answered. They instinctively erased the boundaries of the personal and professional. They knew deep in their hearts, consciously or unconsciously, that taking action was beyond roles and responsibilities – it was about duty. With no personal agenda, they became our industry's frontliners.

Looking closely at and into their leadership has the power to help us all learn how to emerge stronger from a crisis, be it personal or professional, by:

- providing examples of courageous leadership that we can relate to
- offering new insights into our own ways of processing and responding to challenges
- building within us an understanding of what inspires us to take personal leadership of ourselves (and even others around us)
- finding ways of controlling natural reactions such as fear, fatigue and loss of faith
- establishing confidence in our ability to face the future
- making the most of the lessons from history, our living history, even those challenging us to unnatural degrees, as recently learned from Mother Nature
- ensuring we do not waste the teacher from our own life history

Importantly, while a chapter has been dedicated to ensuring a degree of understanding around the functioning of the human brain when confronted by a crisis, there can be no exactness in the understanding of how one is able to process the experience of a crisis – no specific start, middle and end – nor how one then makes sense of it all.

Because the fact remains, we are dealing with:

- human lives
- human situations
- human interpretations and emotions
- human variability in individual experience

Each experience is respected for the insight and inspiration it offers, enabling us to accelerate our healing together, moving forward knowing that whatever the next crisis, however we are next challenged, we have insight that can help us come through stronger.

THE WHO

The leaders selected for the interviews were not previously unknown to me. Quite the contrary; we had worked together, we shared summit stages together, struggled to find solutions together, laughed together, debated together and dined together. I watched them during the crisis. I saw first-hand how quietly, consistently, thoughtfully and almost intuitively they pushed past their own fear and found ways of inspiring security, unity, creativity and compassion. Their wiring to lead was evident.

The leaders knew that they would be asked to dig deep in the interviews, to get personal, and I would seek more than had already been extracted from them in the hundreds of interviews they had given during and since the crisis. They knew this was going to be different. Because they knew I knew them, respected them and appreciated who they were as people, not simply professional personalities. And they knew me.

I remain profoundly grateful that these leaders trusted me to tap into their lives, not only their livelihoods, during a challenging, shared chapter in the story of all our lives. The time I spent with them revealed that these leaders experienced the world's shared pandemic in different ways. They offered many different perspectives and many different points of view.

They possessed many different skills and sensibilities that helped them to navigate their way into the eye of the storm using various approaches. Despite their differences, they all shared a common goal of reaching a safe, stable and brighter 'after'.

That said, there were remarkable similarities too. For me personally, one of the most touching parallels was their complete discomfort about being referred to as a 'hero'. Every leader interviewed pushed back when the term was used to describe them.

> *They wore no capes. They sought no audience.*
> *They acted instinctively, immediately and often invisibly.*

The leaders processed events with such speed, strength and certainty that they were not always aware of how their minds were operating. They were able to face the pace and scale of the growing danger, the resulting risks they and others faced, the implications of inaction, what 'safety' looked like, and the decisions they needed to take in the short, medium and long terms.

Every leader stepped forward to lead without a personal agenda or a desire to be identified for their leadership. They just did it. Why? Because they heard a calling, and so, they had to do something. Doing nothing was not an option. It was in their wiring. They did what they felt they could do, in their own way, within their sphere of influence.

For some, doing something meant turning an international convention centre into a temporary hospital, or increasing local municipality bed capacity, or speeding up the vaccination roll-out.

For others, it meant putting on their uniform every day and going to work at their shuttered hotel, keeping up the hopes of reopening once more for guests and staff.

For some, it meant opening up their kitchens to cook millions of meals for frontline medical staff.

For some, it meant creating web programmes to keep students connected, factually informed and motivated about the industry they saw grounded at that time, yet had the potential to recover even stronger.

Meanwhile, some were encouraging their executives to make audio recordings of bedtime stories for staff to play for their children after a long day of working and home-schooling.

And some simply helped their staff set up home offices, creating comfortable, creative, confident spaces for people to remain not only productive but positive.

There were the people who helped their teams find ways to inspire locals to share their favourite places, to share the place they call 'home' with the world, keeping the dream of travel 'one day' strong.

Others held ongoing briefings and shared video messages with their staff across the globe. Not only did these leaders seek to embed an understanding of the need to work as one to take care of the financial health of the business, but they also knew it was important to keep a close eye on the mental health of their business community.

And others, who had gone through crises before, inspired their people to look beyond the 'here and now' to an after, supporting bold imagination with bold investment, ready for when the airport, airline and hotel doors opened once more.

The list goes on and on and on.

Slowly, steadily, and sincerely, we watched these leaders find ways of bringing people in their professional community together in the most trying and traumatic of times, enabling them to find a sense of calm, a sense of confidence, a sense of purpose and a sense of hope. How was it that they were not only able to find the eye of the storm but were willing to guide others to it and through it to safety? How were they able to remain clear, confident and hopeful? Their experience is important to us and this is exactly why this book was written. Through understanding how these leaders were able to find the personal strength to calmly step forward and lead through a crisis, we can understand the thought processes and actions of ourselves and others. We can learn to step forward as individuals and as a collective. Most importantly, we are able to honour this human truth:

> *In a crisis no one, absolutely no one,*
> *should be left to stand alone.*

So, who were the people I wished to include in this book?

The twenty carefully selected leaders in this book helped me understand how our hearts and brains work in a time of crisis. Through sharing their experiences, they showed me:

- how we process information differently during a crisis
- the mental behaviours and states that frequently emerge during a crisis
- how psychological effects are different in each phase of a crisis
- how to communicate effectively during these changing states of mind,

and importantly,

- how to use crises from our past as a way of strengthening our ability to bravely take on, and calmly make it through, crises in our present and future.

They were leaders we were used to seeing all suited up, often seen in the headlines as award winners, MOU signers, VIP listers, media quote givers. Industry champions and thought leaders. Colleagues, and importantly, trusted friends.

Suddenly, and in some cases to our surprise, they were the industry's frontliners, unable to sit and wait for someone to do something. They responded instinctively to 'the moment' without a personal desire to make it '*my* moment'. Knowing them, respecting them, wanting to learn from them and knowing they would trust me to get the most and best out of them, they became the focus of this literary labour of love.

So, who said 'yes'? Who answered the calling for an interview? Here is a summary of the leaders chosen to be a part of this book, with a brief outline of who they are, how I am connected to them and the extraordinary leadership they exhibited.

Please note full professional profiles can be found in Chapter 15.

AVIATION LEADERS

WILLIE WALSH, DIRECTOR GENERAL, INTERNATIONAL AIR TRANSPORT ASSOCIATION (IATA)

For any travel and tourism practitioner like myself, it is important to understand the aviation link in the travel experience chain. Aviation is the primary artery of global travel, tourism and even trade. It keeps the heartbeat of the global economy and community strong. Ask anyone to name one of the most important leaders in global aviation and they will say, Willie Walsh. From their Geneva headquarters, IATA represents over 300 airlines worldwide that together account for 83% of total air traffic. Willie is one of the most qualified (he is a licensed pilot), active and visible members of the global travel and tourism community. Having known and engaged onstage with Willie for several years, my respect and appreciation for him was already high. It was elevated dramatically when in early 2021 he took the helm at IATA, and I, with others in the global leadership community, watched Willie step forward as one of the most vocal advocates of safety. He smartly broke through barriers to COVID-related travel restrictions and regulations, continuously, tirelessly (and often bullishly) working across the global travel, tourism and trade ecosystem to help governments understand what was needed to restart global aviation and therefore the global economy. This work included the development of innovations, such as the IATA Travel Pass, that elevated traveller confidence by making essential travel information and personal data more accessible and manageable in even the most complex of times. At the same time, Willie pushed back on costly COVID-19 testing that added prohibitive time and cost to traveller movement. Going beyond the pure aviation link in the travel chain, Willie focused on the strength, safety and smoothness of the entire chain. He knew exactly what he was doing, why, who needed to help make it happen and how it was going to be of benefit to all.

PAUL GRIFFITHS, CEO, DUBAI AIRPORTS AUTHORITY (DAA)

'Staggering' is one of the only ways to describe the vision, courage, speed, scale, creativity and quality of delivery at Dubai International Airport (DXB), one of the world's largest and busiest airports that served over eighty-six million international passengers in 2019. It's also one of the most awarded and admired airports in terms of turning inspiring ideation into invaluable economic, social and environmental impact. Paul became CEO in 2007 and has been greatly respected for leading DAA's operations and developments. But his mandate is not limited to DXB. He is also responsible for Dubai World Central (DWC) which will have a capacity for over 160 million passengers once completed. Altogether, Paul's portfolio reaches over one-third of the world's population within four hours of flying. Paul and I have shared many a think tank, stage, conversation and social connection over the years; he is a leader I have always looked to as a case study. The creativity, courage, excitement and class with which he leads such global infrastructure and operations is truly breath-taking. Under Paul's leadership, DAA became a global benchmark in safe, steady passenger service and staff job protection, with a successful reopening during the pandemic and repeated reinvention of airport operations. Despite the grounding caused by COVID-19, Paul kept staff, ideas, hope and innovation moving, working with his stakeholders, staff community and partners to transform the airport into a new model for traveller experience, and importantly, one of the earliest airports worldwide to reopen smoothly and safely during the crisis, with new ways of delivering traveller experience excellence in mobility and hospitality, and with no losses of jobs or hope.

HOSPITALITY LEADERS

MALCOLM HENDRY, MANAGING DIRECTOR, RED CARNATION HOTEL COLLECTION

A lifelong hotelier, Malcolm is Managing Director of Bbar, as well as London's The Rubens at the Palace, Hotel 41, and Edinburgh's 100 Princes Street, three of the globally admired and awarded boutique hotels in the family-owned and run Red Carnation Hotel Collection, which operates eighteen exceptional hotel properties worldwide. Having known Malcolm for over a decade, including over a dozen visits to his beautiful boutique properties, I can firmly attest to him being an active embodiment of the company's promise 'no request too large, no detail too small'. I was taken aback to see Malcolm's leadership during the pandemic as he provided guests, partners and staff with a tireless example of hospitality in its truest form as a verb, not only a noun. Lockdown after lockdown, month after month, even when there were no international travellers arriving, no bookings mounting, no doormen present to welcome the world to two of London's finest five-star boutique hotels, Malcolm was walking the hotel halls in his uniform, keeping the hearts of his staff, and the brands, beating strong. Taking global sales calls from the hotel lounge, he showed the world that while the doors may be closed, the cocktail lounge candles are still burning, the flowers on the piano are still fresh and the hope of guests returning from across the world is still strong. Because that's what he, as a leader, felt he was called to do.

MARLOES KNIPPENBERG, CEO, KERTEN HOSPITALITY

So many in the hospitality industry know Marloes Knippenberg as '*that* woman CEO' topping industry CEO lists, power lists and women in leadership lists. But anyone who knows Marloes knows she is grateful for these honours, but she is not defined by them. I am blessed to be one of those people. From the moment I met Marloes online on RISE, the web-programme I created with Professor Demian Hodari (another interviewee), I knew she had great credentials and character. Her portfolio of properties grew dramatically during the crisis and in this book I wanted to explore how she was able to sustain growth and deliver under the direst of circumstances. What I was not aware of until our interview for this book was how bravely she alone led her global team through some of the darkest days of the hotel industry. As demonstrated through her leadership during the early days of COVID-19, Marloes's values were on the front line more than on the front cover. Which is exactly why, when the world was shutting down, she chose to be at work rather than in her home with her creature comforts. Today her leadership remains the fuel of exceptional business and team growth. Championing over fifty development projects across twelve or more countries, Marloes is recognised as one of the industry's most innovative developers of spaces. Marloes brings to the industry a unique combination of not only vision, creativity, expertise and style, but a commitment to ESG-based business growth for the people and places connected to Kerten.

PUNEET CHHATWAL, CEO AND MANAGING DIRECTOR, INDIAN HOTELS COMPANY LIMITED (IHCL)

When I reflect on the global pandemic, one of the people I thank for sharing a particularly touching story of a company that heard its call to leadership is Mumbai-based Puneet Chhatwal. A colleague with whom I have enjoyed many debates and discussions around the world on conference stages, around think tank tables and over business dinners, Puneet leads the IHCL, which operates over 250 hotels and forty-three restaurants in over ten countries and directly supports over 28,000 employees. He holds close to his heart IHCL's legendary Taj Hotel brand, which proudly represents a portfolio of luxury properties, including some of India's most iconic palaces. Puneet is respected and applauded globally as one of the industry's finest leaders. Impressive? Yes, but that is not why he is part of this book. During the early days of the pandemic when Puneet and I were backstage (virtually), Puneet shared an incredible, little-known story about how the Tata family's Taj Public Service Welfare Trust (TPSWT) showed the hospitality industry what true 'hospitality' means: caring for frontliners by providing them with a 'home' when they were unable to go home. Under Puneet's quiet, humble, yet hugely effective, championing of one of India's most highly recognised and respected family trusts TPSWT provided over six million meals and 125,000 bed nights at Taj hotel properties to medical frontliners across India between early 2020 and the end of 2022. In doing so, Puneet, Taj Hotels, IHCL and the TPSWT inspired hotels and restaurants across the country to step up and support the effort through donations or even direct bed and meal offerings of their own. Brilliant.

GOVERNMENT LEADERS

HON. PREMIER ALAN WINDE, PREMIER OF THE WESTERN CAPE, SOUTH AFRICA

A leader I have had the honour of knowing personally as a government official, stakeholder, colleague and friend for over a decade when I lived in South Africa's fairest Cape province (also one of the world's most sought-after tourism destinations), Hon. Premier Winde is one of the most trusted political figures in the nation. His determination to cut through red tape to ensure the delivery of essential services to the province's seven million residents has earned him respect. His mission is clear: ensuring that every single day is used for 'improvement of economic and household prosperity by getting the basics right, such as education and healthcare, and improving safety and public transport for all the residents of our province'. This includes being honest about where improving the efficiency of government service delivery is needed, and where innovation and new technology can be introduced to make a meaningful, sustainable difference. During the pandemic Hon. Premier Winde applied these principles to tackle wave after wave of the pandemic with exceptional courage, creativity and humanity. Hon. Premier Winde is a firm believer in the power of innovation, collaboration and delivery, especially in times of challenge when he believes creativity and connectivity is at its best. The immense respect that people in both the public and private sectors have for him unlocked his ability to bring people and ideas together to deliver several critical initiatives with exceptional speed and scale. These initiatives included transforming Cape Town's international convention centre into first, a hospital of hope, and then, a municipal vaccination centre – two high-visibility, high-impact projects vital to sustaining the confidence and hope of citizens across the city and province. He is one of those leaders that you can call in the middle of the night if you are in trouble and they will answer the call.

HON. NAJIB BALALA, FORMER MINISTER OF TOURISM AND WILDLIFE FOR KENYA

A colleague and client for many years and over many milestones in global travel and tourism sector growth, development and crises, Hon. Minister Balala is one of the sector's most trusted and respected government leaders. He served as Cabinet Secretary for three different terms since 2008 and led the travel and tourism industry recovery following several terror-related crises. Hon. Minister Balala holds the record for being the longest-serving leader of Kenya's tourism and wildlife portfolio. The combination of his strong strategic acumen in policy development as well as exceptional, on-the-ground appreciation for excellence in tourism experience delivery, earned him a reputation as one of the most approachable, accountable, solutions-driven leaders in the tourism sector globally. This reputation was reinforced when he was elected chairperson of the United Nations World Tourism Organization's (UNWTO) executive council. Importantly, during the global pandemic Najib activated his exceptional industry experience, expertise, network, reputation and credibility to immediately align the Kenyan tourism industry at home, while connecting destination Kenya to critical intelligence, innovation and decision-making globally. The country's president confidently and visibly supported Najib's leadership as he consistently positioned the safe restart and recovery of travel and tourism as core to the well-being of Kenyans across the country and across all industries, embedding the travel and tourism sector as a national priority, its recovery a national imperative. Kenyans got it, and they worked together to get it done. Najib has the unique ability to hear his calling with exceptional speed and strength, as well as tireless dedication, loyalty and humility. Wearing his signature bow tie, Najib has shown he will do everything in his power to protect his beloved Kenya and Kenyans.

GLOBAL TRAVEL BUSINESS LEADERS

GAVIN TOLLMAN, CEO, THE TRAVEL CORPORATION (TTC)

A proud son of Africa living his life's passion for travel, Geneva-based Gavin is CEO of The Travel Corporation (TTC) a global travel company that is family run and operated. It comprises forty award-winning travel brands responsible for carrying over two million travellers a year to over seventy countries worldwide. And yet I, and all who know him, know that he always wears the incredible achievements of his family's business with grace and gratitude. Gavin embraces his leadership role as an immense responsibility. As a result, with more than thirty years of proven experience and expertise in the global travel, tourism and hospitality industry, Gavin applies his innate sensitivity towards the desire of travellers to get up close and personal with the people and places they visit. Having worked with Gavin and his remarkable family for fifteen years, I can attest to his achievement of becoming one of the first business leaders in global hospitality firmly committed to making travel matter for both the visitors and the visited of the places touched by TTC's brands, businesses and teams. This commitment has been at the heart of TTC's not-for-profit TreadRight Foundation for fifteen years and across over sixty active, measurable projects worldwide focused on cultural, social, economic and environmental sustainability. Gavin personally acknowledged the trust that a world of travellers and TTC staff have in the brands of his family's business. As soon as the global pandemic started to ground the world, Gavin mobilised his company's global network to ensure the safe passage and repatriation of thousands of stranded guests on tours across the world. As the world began to slowly reopen to travel, Gavin championed TTC's creation of well-being directors on all its guided tours – a powerful idea that brought not only best-in-class healthcare, aligned to the World

Health Organization's (WHO) guidelines for travellers and staff, but also invaluable peace of mind. Priceless.

MATTHEW UPCHURCH, CEO, VIRTUOSO

A greatly valued colleague within the global tourism leadership community and champion of keeping the heart and humanity of travel strong, Matthew is recognised and respected as one of the leaders in connecting over 20,000 of the world's knowledgeable and capable travel advisors with millions of excited luxury travellers across the globe. US-based Matthew is a firm advocate of ensuring that human connections make a lasting, meaningful impact on both the visitor and the visited. Celebrated by the global travel industry, Matthew always firmly places his visionary eyes and heart on creating a better tomorrow through travel. During COVID-19, Matthew's belief in the human spirit as the basis for stronger global development came to the fore; his tireless effort to maintain his community of travel advisors was an invaluable fuel to help the industry move forward with confidence and connection. In particular, Matthew embedded in each member of the immense Virtuoso network just how important they are to the future of travel. Matthew played a vital role in travellers revaluing the work of travel advisors, as clients sought the confidence and reassurance that their travel decisions were the right ones, and that they are never alone if anything goes wrong, especially unexpected changes in travel regulations, airline and airport operations. During the crisis and since then, Matthew looked to new opportunities for industry growth as a lever for the sector's economic recovery, as a global platform for meaningful, equitable, inclusive job creation, and as a way of keeping people across the world understanding and caring for one another.

GEOFFREY KENT, FOUNDER AND OWNER, ABERCROMBIE & KENT (A&K)

There is no question about it, when it comes to identifying the pioneer of luxury travel, true luxury travel, there is only one name: Geoffrey Kent. A loved colleague and friend for many years and a gentleman recognised and celebrated across the global industry, Geoffrey was the visionary of luxury adventure travel back in 1962 when he and his parents established Abercrombie & Kent (A&K). It became a brand synonymous with luxury touring and expeditions at their finest. Importantly, Geoffrey was the first to champion the principle that wildlife should only be shot with a camera, never with a gun, creating the first African photographic safaris in the 1960s. Since then, he has inspired and delivered innovative approaches to enable travellers to see the world's most remarkable destinations and feel the heartbeat of their people through his A&K brand, while making a meaningful impact on local communities, environments and economies through A&K Philanthropy. Today A&K's award-winning travel services extend around the globe to more than a hundred countries on all seven continents serving 30,000 guests per year. Despite being respected as an elder of the global tourism community, his youthful spirit, endless reserves of energy and enduring love of discovering the world's great gifts of people and places continues to see Geoffrey actively committed to the business. And the A&K brand still carries Geoffrey's commitment to ensure each and every client enjoys the most inspirational experiences in the world – journeys that are awe-inspiring, exciting, intriguing, rejuvenating and memorable. The global pandemic was not Geoffrey's first major crisis; his business has endured crises at a local, regional and global scale before. This experience alongside his innate sense of vision, immensely creative spirit and acute understanding of what his guests want (sometimes even before they can articulate it) made Geoffrey an important leader to include in this book.

DARRELL WADE, CHAIRMAN AND CO-FOUNDER, INTREPID

Long before 'sustainability' became an industry buzzword, and subsequently the basis of leadership discussions and debates, Darrell Wade was showing a world of travellers how to enjoy sustainable travel in the right way, in the right places, for the right reasons. This is exactly why his leadership has been needed right now. Australia-based Darrell now stands (over six feet!) tall as one of the champions of the future of tourism in a post-COVID-19 world. As co-founder of Intrepid, Darrell has run the company for more than twenty years; he is now not only the group's chairman, but also a widely respected industry entrepreneur and sustainability advocate, reinforced by his positions as Vice Chair of the World Travel & Tourism Council (WTTC) and chair of the WTTC sustainability committee. During the pandemic I, along with others across the tourism world, observed and applauded Darrell. He was always the (sometimes all alone) voice in the (virtual) room reminding leaders of not only the enormous responsibility, but the incredible opportunity they faced. Darrell claimed they must rebuild the travel and tourism industry in a truly sustainable way, not just because it was the right thing to do, but because it was the smart thing to do! His leadership in sustainable tourism development and his business's proof of delivery, long before the pandemic and before 'sustainability' became part of the industry's vernacular, has established Darrell's company as the global benchmark and go-to for business solutions that benefit the planet, brand and bottom line all at once.

CYRIL RANQUE, FORMER PRESIDENT, TRAVEL PARTNERS GROUP, EXPEDIA

Having interviewed Cyril as part of a different initiative during the early days of the pandemic, it was clear that he was a man not just wired, but consciously built to lead through crisis. As the president of Travel Partners Group when COVID-19 emerged, Cyril knew exactly what to do to protect Expedia's people, position and partners as booking cancellations started to pour in the moment news of border and sky closures occurred. For more than fifteen years he led Expedia, a global travel search and booking platform firmly at the forefront of using the power of technology to unlock the world of travel and recognised for having the broadest offering in the travel industry including over three million properties, over 220,000 unique activities and over 500 airlines, along with dozens of cruise lines and thousands of car rentals. Cyril's role included championing the integration of all travel partners through the marketing, distribution, data and technology solutions of the Expedia Group platform; he also applied his experience, expertise and exceptionally strong spirit towards finding win:win:win solutions, fast. Knowing him and the speed at which he made smart, business- and job-saving decisions, it was imperative to include him as one of the leaders profiled in this book.

DESTINATION LEADERS

JULIA SIMPSON, PRESIDENT AND CEO, WORLD TRAVEL & TOURISM COUNCIL (WTTC)

Without aviation there is no global travel and tourism. When a grounded world needs to find its way back to the runway safely and smoothly, after the industry's biggest crisis of our generation, who better to have at the helm of the global business community than an aviation expert? London-based Julia is head of the WTTC, a global industry body representing over 200 companies and accounting for two-thirds of a trillion US dollars in annual turnover (the equivalent to 30% of the entire sector) and one to which my business is honoured to belong. The WTTC has the world's largest community of C-suite leaders who are committed to shaping a safe, strong and sustainable future for travel. It is a private-sector organisation that is aligned with the public sector. The WTTC's mission is to '*maximise the inclusive and sustainable growth potential of the Travel & Tourism sector by partnering with governments, destinations, communities, and other stakeholders to drive economic development, create jobs, reduce poverty and foster peace, security, and understanding in our world.*'[1] Importantly, 'the council's members are the chairmen or chief executives of leading global travel and tourism companies, from all geographies and industries, including hotels, airlines, airports, tour operators, cruise, car rental, travel agents, rail, as well as the emergent sharing economy, enabling them to speak with one voice to governments and international bodies.' When observing Julia take on this huge role during the crisis it became clear that she brought not just a strong IQ to the industry, but also an exceptional EQ. She knows how important it is to lead with confidence and compassion through a crisis, making sure no one is left behind. Standing at the head of the industry and with grace and poise, Julia is certain of the future of travel and tourism and is always ready to answer the call.

FAHD HAMIDADDIN, CEO, SAUDI TOURISM AUTHORITY (STA)

How does one of the highest profile, most highly scrutinised, highly anticipated and hugely inspiring tourism development nations in the world stay positively and productively focused on delivering its vision when the world has been forced to a standstill? The answer lies in putting in place a leader who not only understands the power of vision to keep hearts and minds creative, productive and connected, but also leads with a unique combination of gravitas and genuineness that inspires others to rise up. Riyadh-based Fahd leads one of the world's boldest destination authorities, STA. It is a national tourism organisation firmly focused on the national, regional and global promotion of Saudi Arabia as the doorway to the authentic warmth, diversity and hospitality of Arabia. I am honoured to call Fahd a colleague and friend. He is a leader with exceptional strengths in marketing and investment and in truly sustainable destination development across economic, social, cultural and environmental imperatives that will make a lasting impact for generations to come. From day one of the pandemic Fahd applied his professional acumen alongside his human understanding to keep the STA community calm, confident and connected, embedding the importance of his team's work in transforming not only the image and economy of destination Saudi, but also the lives and livelihoods of the Saudis. His powerful yet beautifully personal approach made a world of difference in accelerating Saudi's progress in becoming one of the most sought-after destinations in the world for travellers, the travel trade and investors alike.

KIMARLI FERNANDO, FORMER CHAIRPERSON, SRI LANKA TOURISM BOARD

A symbol of the spirit, strength and style of her island nation, Kimarli is a woman who lives her calling. Like all Sri Lankans, she knows well the importance of travel and tourism to their country's economy, community and identity, and how the industry has helped connect the nation to the world following a long, painful civil war fought from 1983 to 2009. All Sri Lankans understand the impact of tourism on their lives and livelihoods, as well as its healing power. That is why Kimarli's leadership of the sector was crucial to inspiring confidence in a safe, secure and hopeful future for the nation's people, in a country where the tourism industry represents over 10.5% of GDP and 10.9% of employment. Elegantly leading Sri Lanka's tourism industry from Colombo from late 2019 to mid-2022, Kimarli applied her exceptional experience and expertise in banking to building a stronger, more results-orientated tourism sector. With over thirty-three years of experience and a proven track record of good corporate governance, ethical practices, effective implementation of new strategies, re-engineering of organisations and her strong stakeholder alignment capabilities, Kimarli has assisted Sri Lankan tourism to recover post-pandemic. Kimarli's appointment came just before the global shutdown, which caused Sri Lanka's economy and people to be traumatised due to the collapse of the travel and tourism industry. She quickly became a member of the Presidential Task Force for the prevention of COVID-19, comprising national, cross-industry, public and private sectors committed to the well-being of citizens and the safe, sustainable reopening of the nation to the world. Through our many shared conversations and (virtual) on-stage appearances during the time, it was clear that her competitive spirit was aglow. Kimarli has always proudly stepped forward for her country, such as when she became the first woman in Sri Lanka to conquer the annual six-mile sea swim, going on to captain Sri Lanka's national swimming team and representing Sri Lanka in the Asian Games. As the first female chairperson to head Sri Lanka's tourism board in the nation's Ministry of Tourism she once again answered the call. I watched and worked alongside Kimarli through the worst of the crisis, continually in awe of her leadership focus, values and determination.

FRED DIXON, CEO, NEW YORK CITY TOURISM + CONVENTIONS

What does it take to lead one of the world's leading tourism destinations – a place where dreams come true for millions of travellers across the globe? A place where when a crisis hits, all eyes are on it as a compass of recovery? A place that connects multiple public and private sector stakeholders, an array of entities and numerous local communities to ensure maximum impact for the good of all the people who call this iconic place 'home'? Fred Dixon! A leadership community colleague and friend for many a year and through many crises, Fred has calmly and capably led New York City as a tourism destination. He has humbly yet powerfully served the travel industry for over thirty years, living and leading through many chapters of growth and crisis. Ever a champion of recognising and activating tourism's wider impact, as President and CEO of the official destination marketing organisation of NYC, Fred's leadership has been integral to the success of the city's tourism economy, especially as the city soldiered through the devastation of COVID-19.

In 2019, NYC hosted over sixty-six million visitors, representing a tenth consecutive annual record. In 2020, that number dropped to 22.3 million. The wider economic impact was a loss of 89,000 jobs. Having led NYC's tourism sector through many crises since joining the organisation in 2005, in the aftermath of 9/11, Fred has unique acumen and sensitivity towards the industry and supports community mobilisation to build a strong, stable and united recovery. For this reason, Fred was central to establishing the Coalition for NYC Hospitality & Tourism Recovery in 2020, bringing together leaders from across the industry to create the project 'All In NYC: The Roadmap for Tourism's Reimagining and Recovery'. It was implemented by the City of New York and supported by a $30 million investment.

What made it possible to bring together so many cross-industry leaders and mobilise recovery efforts so smoothly? It was the trust that these leaders had in Fred. He was a leader who never made success about himself; it was always about New York City and the dream of a better tomorrow. Because if you can recover from a crisis in New York, you can recover from it anywhere.

BRAD DEAN, CEO, DISCOVER PUERTO RICO

If ever there was a leader attuned to the sound of the call to leadership, prepared bravely for a storm, it is Brad Dean. No stranger to crises, San Juan-based Brad has established a reputation across the global tourism industry as one of the leaders you definitely want by your side when Mother Nature has a bad day. Leading the state's destination marketing organisation since 2018, Brad's twenty-plus years of industry experience enabled him to confidently lead the industry and the wider island's community through some of the worst periods of extreme weather in its history. First arriving in Puerto Rico as a financial analyst for General Electric, with several career and geo-position changes thereafter, Brad returned to San Juan to serve his love of the sector, which he also serves in other organisations, including the US Travel Association, Destinations International and Meeting Planners International.

During the pandemic I had the pleasure of being on many of the same (virtual) stages and in many of the same debates around industry trauma and recovery, as Brad. As always, he lived his calling, stepping forward within the global community as an invaluable source of hope, inspiration and idea activation, turning a zero-budget tourism authority into a powerhouse of creativity. As an example, his marketing programmes not only kept travellers across the world dreaming about and planning for their visit to Puerto Rico, but he also encouraged Puerto Ricans to share their favourite locations, experiences and moments with the world. As in the past, through these most recent challenges Brad demonstrated the power of true creativity and community through simple ideas that had a sensational impact, keeping people connected even when they were forced to stay apart, whether across the island or the world.

CRITICAL INDUSTRY PARTNERS

RANI RAAD, FORMER PRESIDENT,
CNN INTERNATIONAL (COMMERCIAL)

The mere mention of his name in the global community commands immense respect and appreciation, yet Rani never seeks to stand tall and boast. On the contrary, his instinct is to bow in humble gratitude, for that is Rani's true character. Yet he is one of the most influential leaders in the global media world, with a firm focus on making a meaningful difference for and with others.

One of the most visionary, bold, creative and compassionate leaders I have ever worked alongside and whom I am blessed to call a friend, London-based Rani spent over twenty-five years as one of the champions of global connectivity through communication. Having begun his career as a researcher at CNN in New York City, his unique combination of vision, courage, ethics and humanity saw him rapidly rise to leadership positions. Most recently, he held the role of President of CNN International Commercial, where he was responsible for CNN International's (CNNI) commercial functions outside the US, along with the development of Turner International's programmatic trading strategy. Celebrated within and beyond the CNN community, in 2013, he ranked seventy-one of 500 in the Arab Business Power List of the world's most influential Arabs. In 2015, he was honoured by the online news portal ArabianBusiness as the thirteenth most powerful Arab aged under forty.

During the pandemic, a time when all but a few travel destinations, brands and businesses were staying off-air and offline, I was fortunate to have a front-row seat watching on (and often working alongside) as Rani activated the network's global reach, trust and creativity to keep travel dreams alive by inspiring people to dream today, travel tomorrow. This included CNNI working with the UNWTO to activate a series of global campaigns and rallying travellers to #TravelTomorrow and #RestartTourism. At the same time, through the intensely demanding pandemic, Rani applied his strengths in human connection towards staying meaningfully connected, one-to-one and one-to-many, to his enormous global CNNIC team and their clients. Tireless and always true, having Rani as part of this book was a given.

DAN RICHARDS, CEO, GLOBAL RESCUE

The industry's greatly trusted and respected first call in times of trouble, Puerto Rico-based Dan founded his company in 2004 – a company that has grown to become the world's leading provider of the medical, security, evacuation and travel risk management services that are needed most by companies, government agencies, NGOs and individuals across the globe. Global Rescue is trusted to provide 'lifesaving integrated medical, security, travel risk and crisis management services, delivered by our teams of critical care paramedics, physicians, nurses and military special operations veterans'. In today's world of global activity, and growing uncertainty, Dan has become the go-to person, especially for travel destinations that recognise the value of emergency response management to deal with any challenges that may occur, whilst ensuring both visitors and the visited alike know that all is being done to maximise safety while minimising risk. As a colleague within the wider industry community, it was clear that Dan's understanding of crisis detection, evaluation, reaction and recovery is world leading, and his approach to leadership is a prime example of grace under fire. Having his involvement in this project was vital to delving deeper into the crisis management process, operationally and psychologically.

PROFESSOR DEMIAN HODARI, PROFESSOR OF CORPORATE STRATEGY, EHL HOSPITALITY BUSINESS SCHOOL, LAUSANNE

It was a connection made a few years pre-pandemic, but it turned into a trusted partnership as soon as the pandemic began. Why and how? Tens of thousands of students and graduates across the global travel, tourism and hospitality academic community were watching their future industry of employment come crashing down. They needed a safe place to be able to separate the news from the noise, honestly and safely ask their questions, exhale . . . and maybe even have a spirit-lifting laugh. And so, in early 2020 Demian and I felt and responded to this calling, co-creating and co-hosting 'RISE' (WWW.RISE-WEEKLY.COM), the travel, tourism and hospitality industry's longest running, global web show that ended up running from 2020–2022 (two years, four seasons, fifty-four episodes). Along with an array of exceptional, inspiring industry leaders, Demian and I discussed how our industry was making sense of each 'next normal' stage in the COVID-19 world, keeping our audiences inspired about the future of our industry – one that we all knew would recover to be, once again, a force for global unity, stability, and importantly, career opportunity. Lausanne-based Demian already had been inspiring students at undergraduate and graduate level for almost a quarter of a century, through his immersive, innovative approach to teaching, delivering executive education courses and facilitating strategic management workshops for hotel companies worldwide. He is respected for teaching over 3,500 industry executives, his research on the strategic relationships between hotel general managers, owners and management companies earning him EHL Researcher of the Year. When I contacted Demian about this book he knew I was calling because I had heard a calling, just as he had heard his.

And so, one by one these twenty leaders shared the realness of their experiences and the richness of their insights, turning up the volume on their inner voices to tell their stories.

THE HOW

Establishing the *who* was one thing. The *how* – getting the leaders to agree to a project that required them to reveal parts of themselves and their lives that they normally keep out of the public arena – was another. But I had to ask. And somehow, somewhere in my heart, I knew they would say yes.

Through direct, personalised email outreach the invitation was extended. The 'ask'? Their time, and their trust, for a one-on-one video interview examining their leadership experience of the global pandemic especially in the early days of the crisis. I had to take each of the leaders back in time in a way that released the rawness of emotion, the flicker of anxiety and sense of urgency that they had felt.

Interviewing on video allowed me to not only listen to what they said, but see *how* they said it – the communication expressed through their body language. The latter offered a key aspect to the analysis of the interviews.

I wanted each leader to share their personal perspective on three critical phases.

Firstly:

- When did they realise something was very wrong?
- What was their understanding of the immediate threat?
- What did 'safety' mean?
- What were their first priorities?
- What did they view to be their responsibility?

Secondly:

- What did they view to be the wider, longer-term implications of the threat?
  - as a society
  - as an industry
  - as a business
  - as a community
- Who was looking to them for safety?
  - above them
  - below them
  - around them
- Where was leadership needed?
- What would happen if they did not step forward?

And thirdly:

- How did they view their leadership during the defining moments of the crisis?
- What motivated them?
- What personal learnings have they gained from that time?
- How do they put that time in perspective?

Established relationships aside, how was it possible to unlock such personal reflection so quickly and safely? It was all about the stimulus put forward to provoke the desired depth of response.

At the beginning of each interview, once initial protocols were observed, a carefully crafted, highly sensory three-minute video was played for the interviewee. It was a video montage of milestones from January 2020 to mid-2021. The stimulus was raw – it had been lived through before. In a mere 180 seconds, the video immediately transported the interviewees back to a time when they, like everyone else in the world, were trying to understand what in the world was going on.

The storyline – a media-based look back at the first year of COVID-19 – was straightforward: the first days of the virus being detected in Wuhan, China forcing rapid lockdown; the spread of the virus from China to other parts of the world; the WHO declaring the virus to be a global pandemic; global lockdowns; wave after wave of the virus; discovery of a vaccine; roll-out; countries reopening. Visuals and video clips were taken mainly from global news networks as they communicated to the world the state of the world. Again, nothing not seen before, but something definitely not seen by interviewees for at least two years, and something they hoped never to see again.

As important in the 180 seconds of rewind was the non-visual stimulus, especially the sound: the pace of news reports, of people speaking, sharing their rapid, late-night escape from Wuhan before lockdown; the serious tone of news anchors across the globe reporting on the spread of the virus and impact on lives and livelihoods; official voices of medical experts speaking about the severity of the crisis and lack of global response; the excitement of reporters celebrating airports opening; vaccines being manufactured and administered; enduring voices of concern reminding us that we all need to get through this shared, global crisis; and a closing message asking us what Mother Nature gave us through this challenging time.

Digging deep into their conscious and subconscious thought processes, each leader was taken on a personal, emotionally unfiltered journey, returning them to the moment when they understood that something was different about the threat they faced.

I needed to unlock their memories as real moments in time, including the rawness of sensation that they experienced, including the shock, disbelief, adrenaline, fear, sense of urgency and the need to do something. I needed to dig deep into their conscious and subconscious thought processes, giving a voice to their hearts, not only their heads.

And so, I asked ten questions aimed at gaining valuable insight, not only information, about:

- their awareness as the crisis was unfolding
- their leadership response in pandemic and in past crises
- learnings that emerged from the crisis about leadership and about themselves

Through this one-on-one interview process, the leaders gave me valuable insights. This enabled me to extract rich and solid leadership direction and inspiration that we can all use to move forward in challenging situations. It also helps us determine, often in a whisper to ourselves, 'What do I do now?', helping us to be more confident and compassionate for whatever we may confront in the future.

> *The revisiting of sound and sight unlocked deep emotion, immediately erasing the line between personal and professional. They were just one of the eight billion people in the world watching the world starting to shake.*

Through their experiences, their decisions and their actions, we gain a unique understanding of leadership and these leaders.

A VERY SPECIAL EXTRA VOICE

In addition, this book is honoured to have the contribution of a leader to whom I turned daily during the crisis, albeit on my television and online. He was for me a primary source of information that I trusted, inspiration I could turn to, and on some days, much-needed context and calm I could rely on: Dr Sanjay Gupta, CNN's Chief Medical Correspondent. A practising neurosurgeon, Sanjay also, as the global news network puts it: 'plays an integral role in CNN's reporting on health and medical news for all of CNN's shows domestically and internationally'. Every day through the pandemic Dr Gupta would speak to CNN's world of literally hundreds of millions of often anxious viewers, providing them with updates on the pandemic, and how they could make their lives healthier, more peaceful and more hopeful through the months and months of waiting, watching and worrying.

In the final stages of development of this book, and as the clock ticked down to manuscript submission, I reached out to Dr Gupta (to whom I was a stranger barring our connection through a mutually respected and adored colleague, Rani Raad, referenced above) with a big ask – a wish, really: please would he examine the premise of the book and help me push the thinking? With incredible generosity of time and spirit, he said 'yes'. I am deeply, deeply grateful that he 'showed up'. In so doing he has provided exceptional richness of wisdom and warmth to the pages that follow and the learnings that are revealed.

The Call to Leadership embodies a hope that we use the time that Mother Nature gave us to ensure we all are stronger together, whatever is ahead of us. It is also a salute to the leaders and unsung heroes around us who simply wanted to ensure that we never lost hope.

CHAPTER 2

TRUE NORTH: LEARNING FROM THE LIVES OF LEADERS

One of our senior leaders of our board, a senior leader in the industry in New York, called me on Wednesday night, about ten o'clock. We were working around the clock at that time. And he said, 'For all of us, there are moments in our lives when we have to step up, and this is your moment, and you're stepping up. You're going to look back on this moment and you're going to be glad that you were in it.'
And he said, 'Everything you've done in your life has led you to this moment and this is why you're here. And this is why your board is behind you.'

FRED DIXON, CEO, NEW YORK CITY TOURISM + CONVENTIONS

Leadership.

We look for it, near and far.

We look up to it, past and present.

We cannot deny we need it, an anchor when there is the threat of a storm.

We learn from it, good and bad.

And when we observe it at its best, we never forget it.

Leadership is one of the most actively sought-out areas of study across the world. Without question, whether for professional or personal reasons, the quest for strengthening knowledge in leadership is global.

Why is there such an interest in leadership?

There are many reasons, and they all lead towards its essence: the study of leadership is a powerful platform for people to develop themselves. Even if we are not currently in a leadership position, leadership is still a topic of great interest because of the lessons it offers us for:

- Professional development: to improve skills that are important to advance our career, such as communication, teamwork and decision-making.
- Personal growth: to help us gain a higher degree of self-awareness of what we value, our sense of purpose, our desire to make an impact and our aspirations to become more.
- Motivation: hearing about the lives and life lessons of others that inspire us to dream bigger, work harder and achieve bolder and brighter.
- Connection: by strengthening our understanding of how to engage more effectively with others in our work and/or personal lives and becoming more through stronger relationships.

As an industry, growth in the leadership sector is quite extraordinary, and quite natural as individuals and organisations seek to unlock and benefit from their own growth and that of others in our increasingly interconnected world. Leadership is even more crucial as we face times of increasing personal or professional challenge.

The leadership industry includes a wide-reaching range of products and services, all looking to make us better people, professionals and drivers of positive change. From on-site to online training and development programmes, to coaching, consulting and publishing, the opportunities for people to unlock growth within themselves and their spheres of influence are endless. And as technology magnifies the power of reach for leadership learning tools, those seeking to spread their knowledge and wings are blessed with an abundance of insight and inspiration.

The publishing industry (including audiobooks and podcasts) provides some of the most time-, cost- and access-efficient ways for individuals to gain new insights, develop new skills and grow both personally and professionally. In 2022 alone, the global corporate leadership training market was estimated to be growing at almost 8% year on year, sustaining momentum towards 2026 to reach a staggering $26 billion. On average, an estimated 4.8 million books are written about leadership per annum, according to the market research agency Technavio.[2]

So, what are people reading? Who is leading the leadership narrative? As our world evolves societally, economically and spiritually, so do our needs in leadership learning. In the twentieth and twenty-first centuries, several leaders emerged. Their books have become, for many of us, our 'Leadership Bibles' (or similar books of great meaning in other faiths). Their theses act as a valuable reflection of the values of the times in which they were first published and are vital resources for understanding leadership and decision-making.

To truly comprehend what makes a great leader, we must explore and learn from the lives of those who have achieved greatness. For this reason:

> *Some of the greatest lessons in leadership come*
> *from understanding the lives of great leaders themselves.*

The biographies and autobiographies of iconic leaders of our times have provided some of the richest insights into the minds, and even hearts, of leaders facing extreme crises. In all cases, they are crises of a political nature:

- British Prime Minister Winston Churchill was saluted for his service as the nation's leader twice, first in 1940–1945 and again from 1951–1955.
- Indian lawyer and civil rights leader Mahatma Gandhi was a definitive figure in the liberation of India from British rule in the 1940s until his assassination in 1948.
- Abraham Lincoln was president of the United States of America from 1861 until his assassination in 1863.
- John F. Kennedy was another president of the United States of America from 1961 until he was also assassinated in 1963.
- American activist and Baptist minister Martin Luther King Jr. was at the heart of the nation's civil rights movement from 1955 until his assassination in 1968.
- Nelson Mandela was South Africa's first freely elected black president, whose long walk to freedom galvanised the nation and world around democratic rule. His leadership from 1994–1999 was a symbol of possibility.

Remarkable, world-connected and impacting lives also worth learning from, who are all personal favourites, include:

- Her Majesty Queen Elizabeth II, who served the United Kingdom and Commonwealth with strength, solidity, lifelong commitment and grace from 1952–2022.
- Sheikh Rashid bin Saeed Al Maktoum, the visionary vice president and second prime minister of the United Arab Emirates, is recognised as the transformational ruler of Dubai from 1958–1990.
- Brazilian national and United Nations humanitarian Sérgio Vieira de Mello was one of the UN's strongest and most inspiring diplomats and programme leaders, whose life ended abruptly in Baghdad in a 2003 UN HQ bombing.
- His Majesty King Hussein bin Talal was leader of the Hashemite Kingdom of Jordan during one of the Middle East's most definitive periods of 1952–1999.

- Lee Kuan Yew was Singapore's first prime minister from 1959 −1990 and the statesman saluted as the architect of the modern island nation.
- Army officer, diplomat and statesman Colin Powell served as US secretary of state over the period of 2001–2005.

All the above, and so many more, have life stories that leave us as readers not only more informed about their courageous leadership journeys during critical times in history, but also inspired by their purpose-driven leadership spirits.

Then there are those who provide leadership lessons through the actual study of leadership. In the twentieth and twenty-first centuries a number of names became regarded as authorities in the study and analysis of leadership – names that no doubt will make you think 'Oh yes, I remember that!'. In the twentieth century this list includes:

- Ken Blanchard, co-author of *The One Minute Manager* and other titles aligned to the same sentiment, such as *Leadership and the One Minute Manager* and *The Servant Leader*.
- Stephen Covey, author of *The 7 Habits of Highly Effective People*. Even since his death in 2012, his most successful contribution to the world's leadership library continues to leave a strong legacy.
- Peter Drucker, author of many titles, including *The Effective Executive* and *Managing Oneself*, is widely regarded as the 'father of leadership'.
- Tom Peters is best known for the seminal book he co-wrote, *In Search of Excellence*, which is often referred to as the best business book of all time.
- Jim Collins, a personal favourite of mine, is the celebrated author of, amongst other titles, *Good to Great* and *Built to Last*, two books that provided global business leaders with insight into 'what makes great companies tick'.[3]

These leaders, and their leadership theories, are a valuable reflection of the desire of organisations and other leaders seeking to maximise productivity and competitiveness through not only the IQ (intelligence quotient – a measurement of a person's intelligence) of individuals and teams but also the EQ (emotional quotient – a measurement of a person's emotional intelligence and ability to understand their emotions and the emotions of others). At the end of the twentieth century, the presence of SQ (spiritual quotient – the sum of a person's IQ and EQ that recognises people are spiritual in nature) started to creep into leadership theories. The high-performance culture was evolving to recognise our need for working not just productively but *purposefully*.

The twenty-first century has seen leading leadership thinkers, authors and coaches championing the need for leaders to look within to unleash their full potential for the benefit of themselves and others. Most notably, these include:

- Angela Duckworth, an author known for her exploration of the human drive to unlock inner strength for leadership excellence, emphasises this concept in her best-selling book *Grit: The Power of Passion and Perseverance*.
- Daniel Goleman is a leadership thinker who firmly anchors his theories in the power of emotional intelligence, as shared in his books *Emotional Intelligence* and *Primal Leadership*.
- Simon Sinek was one of the first thought leaders to emphasise the importance of having a purpose at the core of any leadership journey. His best-selling book *Start with Why* beautifully articulates this important evolution in leadership development.
- Brené Brown is a leadership practitioner and authority valued for encouraging and empowering people to find their strength by showing their vulnerability. She expands professional leadership learning into personal growth through her books *Dare to Lead* and *Rising Strong*.

It's important not to overlook the valuable personal leadership lessons from voices of authority outside the traditional business and leadership publishing genres. These advocates of personal awareness and development emphasise the role these aspects play in personal leadership. Pre-eminently, Malcolm Gladwell is one of the twenty-first century's most insightful writers in the fields of psychology and sociology. His exceptional understanding of human behaviour, not to mention his ability to articulate how the mind works as a basis of enabling effective communication, makes his series of best-selling books powerful tools for leaders who embrace 'leadership' as both a noun and a verb.

Whatever the motivation, the quest for personal growth through effective leadership is never-ending. Every day, in our own ways, we look for ways to strengthen ourselves. To look at and feel proud of the leader we see within ourselves ultimately creates a higher degree of confidence, resilience and hope in our future being full of immense, positive possibility.

> *While leadership can and is learned through formal channels (books, classes, coaching sessions, tools), we cannot overlook the fact that lessons in leadership also come to us every day in various forms, through various people and in various situations. These learnings can strengthen our ability to be smarter and happier and make a positive impact.*

Leadership lessons may be 'indirect', coming from people within the wider global community. They may be people in our lifetime, from whom we can take significant lessons. They may be leaders in history, the military, science, the environment, culture, sports, the arts, economics, any field of study or industry, anywhere in the world. For whatever reason, we admire them, and they have lessons to be shared.

Equally, 'direct' leadership lessons are there for the taking from people we know and admire within our community. They may be people around us, still walking beside us, or even those who sadly have passed on. They may be close to us through a highly personal context: family, faith, working environments, or social contexts. All these leaders share the ability to teach us lessons in leadership based on what we admire in them, the impact that they have on the world around them, and the way in which they through their example fed our desire to emulate them.

Who and where people look for examples of leadership, therefore, varies dramatically. The scale and scope of leadership influence are not important. The power to lead one person, even oneself, is as important as the power to lead many. Likewise, the structure of the learning can be formal or informal, continuous over an extended period or gained in an instant, especially when it comes to leadership in times of crisis.

LESSONS IN A SPLIT SECOND

An interesting aspect of leadership learning has to do with timing. Typically, we seek out learnings on effective leadership when things are calm, and life is relatively comfortable. We have the space needed to absorb information, gain insights and be inspired. Clarity of mind is present, context is clear and rich reading is easily available. Our mental lenses are set at a wide angle.

We read, watch, listen and learn in anticipation of new injections of insight and intelligence. This is especially the case when respected leaders are the messengers of important messages. The personal example they provide of substance, style and spirit make the learnings richer, more rewarding, more enjoyable and even entertaining.

Thankfully, technology makes it possible to have sage advice at our fingertips on visionary thinking, strategic planning, effective implementation and management of the metrics. These chunks of learning are invaluable and, thankfully, frequently updated to keep our learning fresh and relevant, not to mention relatable. We embrace these leadership lessons confident in the knowledge that one day when we put them to the test, they will advance us professionally. Calmly and quietly we mentally file our notes, putting these learnings to the side, ready to use them as and when we feel they will be of value. However, not all times of learning are as quiet, centred and structured as these.

As we all know, there are times in our lives when learning comes as our wide-angle lenses are rapidly, even aggressively, forced into close-up. These are moments when leadership learnings are acquired through massive, unforgettable, 'once in a lifetime' events that jolt us out of our place of calm.

> *These intensely real moments hit us deeply.*
> *Our emotions are raw, making us feel so alive.*
> *These are moments that can ultimately*
> *define who we are, how we view the world,*
> *and how we choose to engage with it.*

These moments may occur in our professional or personal lives: news of a loss of life, loss of job, loss of a company, loss of a loved relationship, or loss of one's own physical and/or financial health. These moments can be consuming. They can also be terrifying and traumatising. These are the moments that define our leadership DNA. Therefore, when we observe leaders who we admire experiencing something traumatic, especially those we know and trust, there is something very powerful about the lessons they leave behind, that they reveal in their leadership DNA. Somehow, they become credible and compelling to us.

Why is this the case? It is because their lessons penetrate not just our minds but also our hearts. We absorb their experiences with an appreciation for the honesty they convey and the courage they reveal. Learnings of how respected leaders cope with 'once in a lifetime' moments of crisis are, therefore, priceless. Not only do they have exceptional leadership qualities, but they remind us that leaders are also human – they feel fear, loss and pain. At the same time, they hear a calling and respond to the crisis before them. They instinctively respond with courage, strength and faith.

ONCE AND NEVER AGAIN, PLEASE

The context of leadership – when one hears the calling – is critical. This is why we need to rewind and remind ourselves of what was happening back in that 'once in a lifetime' occurrence that stopped our world. The term 'once in a lifetime' is heard frequently and has become a source of dramatic effect. In this case, however, it is accurate, especially for global leaders in the travel and tourism industry.

It all started on 31 December 2019. Around the world, we watched the clocks as the hours, minutes and seconds counted down to midnight. Global media covered celebrations from Asia to the Americas as traditional annual fireworks lit up the sky. Streets were buzzing, bars and restaurants bustling, candles burning, crowds singing, hearts hugging. In many ways, it was a New Year's Eve like so many years before. Although entering the 2020s added extra excitement, extra new-decade hope at the start of a new year, as midnight arrived, it was safely, happily, excitedly predictable.

What no one had predicted was that quietly and with very little attention, a media statement would be released on the Wuhan Municipal Health Commission website in the People's Republic of China reporting a cluster of pneumonia cases. The country office of the World Health Organization (WHO) picked up the alert. The mysterious illness was spreading through the city of over eleven million people. Initially, there was little information. Initially, there was little alarm. The hypothesis at the time? A virus transmission had occurred in a wet market, a type of market that sells fresh products, including meat and produce, and where the slaughtering of live animals occurs on-site as a guarantee of freshness.

What was it about a wet market virus that made it so dangerous for humans? Simply put, wet markets are environments where humans, domesticated animals and wild animals all mix. Highly infectious diseases in animals are easily transmissible from animal to animal; they are also transmissible from animals to humans, who are unable to naturally fight off the resulting, often severe, illnesses.

Red lights were starting to appear, and they had nothing to do with New Year's celebrations. Still, across the globe, no one had any idea what was about to happen. The focus of the world was on the new year ahead.

And then the unimaginable happened.

Within two weeks, on 9 January 2020, the WHO announced that the outbreak was caused by a 'novel coronavirus'. This was serious; very serious. Lockdowns rapidly spread across China during January 2020, beginning with Wuhan. The growing panic was not just due to the virus itself, but also people's fear of being trapped in a location that was soon to be locked down. For the first time in our generation, city after city after city in China was shutting down. One could easily understand that many across the world thought: 'it's fine, a city can lock down. Christmas has just passed. New Year's Eve is over. It's winter – everyone can very comfortably stay indoors and stay apart.'

This scenario was not the case, nor ever is the case, in the first weeks of a new year in China – a time when the country looks forward to its biggest national celebration, and the world's biggest human migration: Chinese New Year. It is a time when families across the country and world come together to celebrate the Spring Festival lasting twenty-three days. Homes are decorated, feasts of traditional foods are prepared, and red envelopes are exchanged. It is a time of beauty, bounty and blessing.

Statistically, the Spring Festival is a time of massive commuting and massive commerce. In 2019, just one year prior to the pandemic, over 415 million visits were recorded to have taken place domestically. Internationally, an estimated 6.3 million people travelled overseas. Most importantly, an estimated 513.9 billion yuan ($76.4 billion) was spent in China over the holiday period. The Spring Festival is a reawakening of the nation, including financially.

When did the world start to look East and see warning signs of red? By late January 2020, spread of the virus was causing such concern at government levels that upcoming travel for Chinese New Year celebrations was suspended, bringing to an abrupt halt all movement of people and profits. This was the first indicator to the global community that something very, very bad was happening. So bad that even China was getting worried.

For leaders in the global travel and tourism industry, lockdowns caused immense concern for several reasons. In the short term, there were concerns about China's ability to control the spread of the virus and keep the rest of the world safe. In the medium term, concern grew around China's ability to continue participating in the global tourism community. How would this be possible if the Chinese people were unable to travel? And even if they could, why would they want to if prejudice from being the source country of the virus meant people did not want them?

As a travel destination, China has developed into an absolute powerhouse since the beginning of the twenty-first century, becoming one of the most attractive places to visit in the world. With over sixty-six million international visitors in 2019, China was firmly on the top of people's destination wish lists, drawing in those who sought a travel experience with an intensity of culture, adventure and exploration. China would unlock an understanding of an ancient civilisation, while at the same time, visitors would feel the pulse of a youthful society excitedly shaping the future.

From an outbound travel perspective, China was central to the world's global travel and tourism economy. In 2019 alone, over 150 million international tourists came from China, representing over 10% of the global travelling population. Revenue generated from outbound Chinese travel was over $277 billion. China topped the list of international travel spending, with expenditure almost twice as much as the US, the second-ranked country on the list. The world needed to connect with Chinese tourists. Similarly, China needed tourism to connect with the rest of the world. Closing borders meant cutting off a lifeline of economic and social exchange for the tourism industry. Industry thought leaders immediately recognised the severity of the risks to the global travel and tourism economy.

As the first month of the new year came to a close, things only got worse. On 30 January 2020, the WHO director-general declared that the growing speed and spread of the outbreak was a public health emergency of international concern (PHEIC), the WHO's highest level of alarm.

The growing momentum of the spread of the virus was matched by the momentum of the spread of panic. Weeks later, countries across the globe were placing extraordinary restrictions on people in a desperate bid to halt the virus's spread. COVID-19 was sweeping through the world from East to West, crippling the global economy to levels exceeding any rate of loss in over a century.

But what exactly was COVID-19? Let's get into the technicalities of the virus for a moment as this is important in understanding just how easily the virus not only spread as an illness, but also as a source of fear. COVID-19 stands for CoronaVIrus Disease of 2019. It is a variation of the coronavirus and therefore linked to the common flu, but as serious as SARS and MERS. Yet COVID-19 was and remains very different from a common flu. As explained at the time by the WHO:

> *Most people infected with the virus will experience mild to moderate respiratory illness and recover without requiring special treatment. However, some will become seriously ill and require medical attention. Older people and those with underlying medical conditions like cardiovascular disease, diabetes, chronic respiratory disease, or cancer are more likely to develop serious illness. Anyone can get sick with COVID-19 and become seriously ill or die at any age. The virus can spread from an infected person's mouth or nose in small liquid particles when they cough, sneeze, speak, sing or breathe. These particles range from larger respiratory droplets to smaller aerosols.*

Central to the unprecedented impact of COVID-19 was the reality of:

- the absence of a proven source of the virus
- very real fears of virus mutation
- a lack of understanding of the virus life cycle
- carriers of the virus being asymptomatic and therefore unknown transmitters of the illness
- the reality of global spread being caused by travel – local, regional and international
- the lack of evidence of vaccine discovery on the horizon
- the limitations of healthcare infrastructure
- the growing numbers of those suffering severe illness and death
- the escalating anxiety of who would be 'next'

Wherever coronavirus spread was detected, the focus shifted to flattening the curve and reducing the R-nought rate (rate of spread of infection) to reduce the risk of overwhelming healthcare systems, thereby reducing the threat of rampant fatalities. While so many had no idea what the metric meant, the term still became commonplace and a common cause for concern.

WILDFIRE

By the end of February 2020, the now-familiar virus was gaining momentum at a rate of speed and spread that exceeded all comprehension. Today it is easy to read this with a sense of calm, carefully considering each word on the page. But at the time, it was terrifying. It was hard to keep up with the headlines and even harder to keep calm. Government leaders rapidly put highly restrictive policies in place. They did what they felt they had to do, closing borders and skies to the extent of blocking even their own nationals from returning home.

The contagion of fear brought the global economic, financial and social ecosystem to a standstill. Government leaders needed to protect the health and well-being of their nationals. There was no management plan for a global pandemic. There was no emergency response mechanism for a highly infectious virus. There was no way of hushing the deafening noise. Wherever they were in the world, government leaders did what they felt was necessary in the immediate term: focus on the health crisis immediately in front of them. They could worry about the economic and social crisis later when they would hopefully be able to understand the scale and severity of the damage. How can you blame them?

On 11 March 2020, the WHO officially declared COVID-19 to be a pandemic. The global cross-sectoral emergency and humanitarian call to action was loud and clear, as Dr Tedros Adhanom Ghebreyesus, the director-general of the WHO, declared:

> WHO has been assessing this outbreak around the clock and we are deeply concerned both by the alarming levels of spread and severity, and by the alarming levels of inaction. We have therefore made the assessment that COVID-19 can be characterised as a pandemic. This is not just a public health crisis; it is a crisis that will touch every sector — so every sector and every individual must be involved in the fight.

By the end of March, cities were locking down worldwide. The WHO's tracking of COVID-19 cases demonstrated the ruthless, agnostic, devastating strength of this new virus. The closure of borders, businesses, institutions, and infrastructure became a contagion in itself.

It is important to mention that at this time, unlike any time in the twenty-first or even twentieth century, a pandemic of misinformation took hold. With so little concrete, verified information initially available from trusted global medical authorities, such as the WHO and the US's Centers for Disease Control and Prevention (CDC), the voice of opinion grew louder and louder. And as they grew, fear also grew stronger. As expressed by Paul Griffiths of DAA:

> *I think the mood changed very dramatically over a very short space of time that this wasn't just going to be ridden out. It wasn't just another flu. It wasn't just another thing that we could just brush off and prescribe a few antibiotics. This was a very different ball game. I also think because of the immediacy of social media and the spread of messaging that it created a different dynamic compared with previous pandemics that we've had.*
>
> *The dynamic it created was a sort of human fear. It spread fear faster than the virus itself spread around the population of the world. And I think that fear actually stoked a lot of responses which were not appropriate.*

The flames of fear grew so loud, intense and overwhelming at a global level that the WHO was forced to step in and make an official statement in September 2020 about the emergence of an 'infodemic' alongside the pandemic.

> *The coronavirus disease (COVID-19) is the first pandemic in history in which technology and social media are being used on a massive scale to keep people safe, informed, productive and connected. At the same time, the technology we rely on to keep connected and informed is enabling and amplifying an infodemic that continues to undermine the global response and jeopardises measures to control the pandemic. An infodemic is an overabundance of information, both online and offline. Mis- and disinformation can be harmful to people's physical and mental health; increase stigmatisation; threaten precious health gains; and lead to poor observance of public health measures, thus reducing their ability to stop the pandemic.*

The appeal for caution was loud and clear, as was the appeal for all communications stakeholders, formal and informal, to manage their messaging with great care.

Nerves were at an all-time high. Trust and confidence in a good outcome were sinking lower and lower. By April, an estimated over 16,000 commercial aircraft were parked on airport runways worldwide. Passenger travel was limited to repatriating stranded nationals and transferring medical personnel and equipment to COVID-19 zones. As transport systems were not able to transport raw materials, finished products and other essential items of the global economy, supporting services and manufacturing plants were forced to close, causing global supply chains to slow down swiftly.

By mid-2020, every country had border restrictions in place. Seeing the published stats brought tears to my eyes: the trauma was official.

Destinations with Travel Restrictions to International Tourism (SOURCE: UNWTO DATA SOURCED BY 15 JUNE 2020)

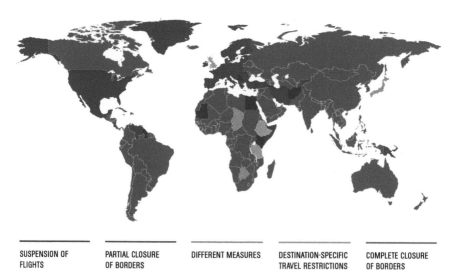

| SUSPENSION OF FLIGHTS | PARTIAL CLOSURE OF BORDERS | DIFFERENT MEASURES | DESTINATION-SPECIFIC TRAVEL RESTRICTIONS | COMPLETE CLOSURE OF BORDERS |

In the final analysis, international tourism declined by 73% in 2020 compared to 2019, a loss of over one billion travellers crossing borders. COVID-19 cost the sector thirty years of growth in just the first year of the crisis. For all of us in the industry, this was unlike anything we could have ever imagined. Our creative minds were unable to calculate such a catastrophe, only Mother Nature had that capability.

Millions of Livelihoods at Risk (SOURCE: UNWTO)

		2019	COVID-19 IMPACT (2020)	2020	2021(E)
✈	INTERNATIONAL TOURIST ARRIVALS	1.5 BILLION	-1.1 BILLION (-73%)	402 MILLION	370-420 MILLION
🚆	TOURISM DIRECT GROSS DOMESTIC PRODUCT (TDGDP)	USD 2.5 TRILLION	-USD 2.0 TRILLION	USD 1.6 TRILLION	USD 1.9-2.0 TRILLION
💲	TOURISM'S SHARE OF WORLD GDP	4.0%	-50%	1.8%	2.0%
🌐	INTERNATIONAL TOURISM EXPORT REVENUES	USD 1.7 TRILLION	-USD 1.1 TRILLION	USD 635 BILLION	USD 700-800 BILLION

In hindsight, these statistics might seem like an interesting way to measure the impact on the industry. But at the time, the reality was that the closures affected all of us around the world.

From the end of 2020, COVID-19 began to mutate, as a virus naturally does. Working through the Greek alphabet, different strains of COVID-19 with varying levels of transmission and damage to those infected were born and named. There were five new variants identified between January 2020 and December 2021 alone. The momentum of mutation kept the world in a state of severe anxiety and governments acted with caution. As a result, with each new strain came a new wave of panic, imposing of border restrictions, creation of travel blacklists, local regulations including lockdowns, and sadly, losses of lives and livelihoods. Over and over and over.

It seemed like life came to a crashing halt in an instant. Our entire way of life – work, school, family dynamics, societal hierarchy, and community relationships – was flipped upside-down by one word that would become colloquial across the world: lockdown. During the initial lockdowns strict measures were imposed worldwide to combat the pandemic. People were told to stay home, stay safe, stay two metres apart, and only go out to buy essential items. Non-essential shops, restaurants and pubs were closed. Places of worship were closed. Outdoor exercise was limited to once a day, initially for only one hour. Police were given enforcement powers.

Neighbours were reporting on each other. The daily rhythm of our lives, including the joy of small, spontaneous moments of contact, connection and conversation with family, friends and strangers alike, stopped. We were asked to focus on the rules, focus on staying safe, and focus on the four walls in front of us.

Still, the virus spread, rapidly and widely. Fear grew as loved ones fell ill and deaths mounted globally. Elderly residents were left alone in care homes, and goodbyes in their final hours were not allowed.

> *The world felt alone, unable to physically connect with those we needed the most. Uncertainty of how long this moment in our lives would last, grew as lockdowns increased and weeks apart turned to months and then years. Patience and prayer had to be endured alone.*

From China to Italy, the UK to the US, and India to Brazil, the world's nations, from East to West, all came to a screeching, earth-pausing halt. There was only one word that adequately described 2020 and has been able to describe every day since: unprecedented. And yet, by the middle of 2020, despite the immense fear, slowly, slowly people began accepting and even embracing the concept of lockdown. As the reality of the situation set in, a sense of almost fascination began to emerge. Almost overnight, the world transitioned from living physically and openly to living virtually. Technology became a secondary life-support system to the recommended, rapidly changing healthcare advice.

How did people stay connected? Skype, then the world's largest web-based digital application for webcam meetings and conferencing, was rapidly challenged by stronger, sleeker, more innovative platforms, including Zoom, Microsoft Teams and Google Meet.

The shift to the digital world happened quickly, and people became increasingly comfortable with sharing their personal lives with even professional acquaintances. Home schooling, work from home, fitness training, team building, medical practising, dance training, life coaching, cooking, personal counselling, concert attending, meeting making, conference networking and other aspects of daily life moved online. This rapid adoption of digital technology allowed people to continue their daily

Weekly Traffic to the Chosen Domains in 2020

(SOURCE: DATA ESTIMATES FROM SIMILARWEB, TRACKS WEBSITE VISITS ONLY.)

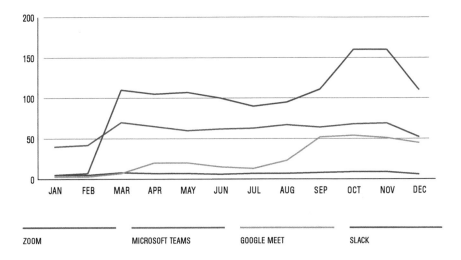

ZOOM — MICROSOFT TEAMS — GOOGLE MEET — SLACK

routines and discover new ways of living virtually. Technology created a myriad of other aspects of the 'new normal' daily life. The five most common words asked on these virtual meeting platforms even today, after all this time? 'Can you hear me now?'!!

Sadly, the realisation of missed milestones also set in, forcing people online for milestones of life, including births, birthdays, engagements, weddings, funerals, memorials and other precious times that should have been able to be shared in person, shared with a hug not a digital heart icon. Our backgrounds, and especially whether our cameras were on or off, became signals of one's state of mind. Much of the cloudiness, confusion and collision of life was reinforced by how we dressed each day, reflecting the split yet singularity in our lives – waist up professional, waist down casual.

As the pandemic continued to impact our daily lives, even the way we communicated with each other changed. A whole new list of acronyms emerged to capture the ups and downs as we moved through lockdown, reopening, lockdown, reopening life from the initial OMG 'Oh My God!' to the more blatant WTF 'What The . . . !' As many of us adjusted to working from home, the term WFH 'work from home', became a common acronym. And for some lucky individuals, the rise of remote work meant that they could even WFA 'Work From Anywhere'. To cope with the stresses of the pandemic, many people adopted a new mantra: PYB 'Pick Your Battles'. These acronyms and others have become shorthand for the extraordinary challenges and changes that we've all experienced over the past few years.

Like the lockdown language we started to use, the methods we used to keep calm, productive, fit and focused on simply getting through, became coping mechanisms and even sources of entertainment. We all remember being sent a link for a Zoom date at which 'quarantinis' were served! Holidaying in the lounge, finding ways of laughing and learning, and making the long periods of lockdown feel shorter and healthier were our new reality and a basis of unity. Even if no one could go anywhere, there were still ways to be together.

The changes to our daily lives and lifestyles had an immediate impact on the economy, affecting both the flow of finances and the structure of supply chains.

> *Lockdown life accelerated innovation and inspired a myriad of business ideas, especially applications, to keep people connected, informed, educated, entertained – and spending!*

The changes have remained to this day as a legacy of these times. Two fascinating examples are clothing and food retail. The unusual nature of the 'new now' in these pandemic times saw the retail sector boom as high street and mall shopping switched to online shopping, as comfy clothing from the waist down became the norm, the perfect work-from-home solution for achieving work-life balance.

Sportswear Companies More Resilient Than Rest of Apparel Industry

(SOURCE: MCKINSEY GLOBAL FASHION INDEX, MARKET CAPITALISATION INDEX DECEMBER 2019=100)

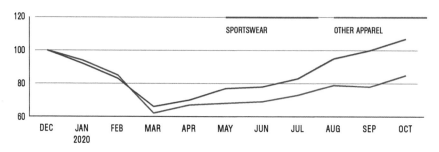

It was a similar trend for food delivery, whether it was fresh groceries or ready-made meals from restaurants unable to open their doors for dine-in service. We all needed what we needed – and now. No one had patience, even though we were going nowhere. Supply chains were immediately impacted. How did distributors cope with demand? They hired quickly as seen in the chart below which focuses on the response of American companies forced into overdrive as a result of the surge in customer demand for at-home delivery. Fascinating to note is the service provider showing the highest rate of growth: Instacart. Who were they? The vast majority of us had probably never heard of them before. Like many, many home-delivery based businesses, the pandemic brought them to life as millions of people went online to see what 'the world's largest online grocery service' had to offer from across its now over 500 million products sourced from over 40,000 stores (ranging from local grocers to national chains), all ready for drop-off at their door in over 5,500 cities across the US and Canada.

Who's Hiring During COVID-19? Number of Jobs Companies Planned to Add Due to Pandemic
(SOURCE: NPR AND MARKET WATCH AS OF 26 MARCH,2020. INCLUDES CONTRACT AND PART-TIME WORKERS.)

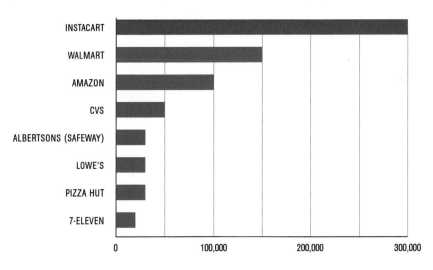

People were buying in because they were staying in. And staying in meant finding ways to stay sane, doing something to pass the time, finding some form of mental escape.

And so again they turned to, and turned on, their screens. Online streaming services, including Netflix, Amazon and others, became daily distractions and addictions.

Number of Paid Netflix Subscribers Worldwide at End of Respective Year

(SOURCE: NETFLIX – UNTIL 2016, CANADIAN SUBSCRIBERS WERE INCLUDED IN THE INTERNATIONAL SUBSCRIBER SEGMENT.)

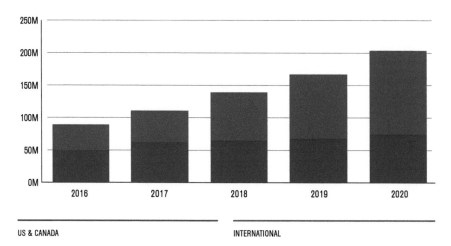

US & CANADA   INTERNATIONAL

Likewise, the demand for fitness products increased as it became clear that the pandemic would be lasting far longer than initially expected. On the other hand, consuming comfort food, especially avocado on soda-bread toast, posed a risk to weight and well-being.

Fitness Apps Saw More Growth Than Wellness Apps (SOURCE: APPTOPIA, STRAVA)

SESSIONS PER WEEK

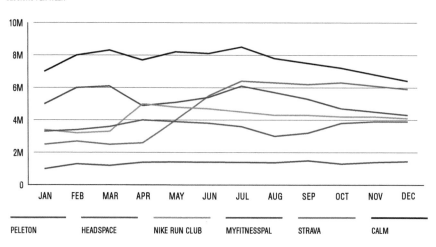

PELETON   HEADSPACE   NIKE RUN CLUB   MYFITNESSPAL   STRAVA   CALM

It seemed to only be getting harder to go out. Restrictions and regulations became more confusing and more frustrating.

No mask? No entry.

No vaccine certificates? No table booking.

No 'fit to fly'? No travel.

No way to get to the shops? No problem – everything you need is only a click away.

Not everyone was stuck inside, however. Interestingly, Mother Nature also got busy, rebooting the world the way she felt it should be. Animals took to city streets, seemingly taking back their land, birds seemed to sing louder, rivers and lakes seemed to flow brighter, and Mother Nature seemed to breathe easier.

Acknowledging the doom and gloom of the pandemic is important because it was the fear, the hostility and the death that changed so much so quickly. As with all times of severe challenge, despite the time away from friends and family, the time children missed out on school and social interactions, the big events missed, we also had some silver linings. One cannot speak about this time without also speaking about the heroes, those who ignored the fear and cared for the sick, kept society moving, and protected their families, communities and employees. They became known as frontliners. These heroes were shining lights in the darkness during the most difficult days of the pandemic. They were the people we clapped for, the people our children drew rainbows for, including:

- doctors who worked 24/7 to see the sea of patients coming through their doors and wards, all struggling to breathe, eyes searching for a way to calm their fears
- nurses who held the hands of the dying while families said goodbye through video calls
- volunteers who put their hands up to do the behind-the-scenes work, keeping places clean and safe, keeping essential workers fed, keeping shelves stocked, keeping medical trials going forward for solutions
- faith leaders sitting with those ill, sustaining their faith . . . or readying them to say 'goodbye'
- teachers who continued going into schoolrooms so that the most vulnerable children had a place to go, and so that those like the nurses could still go into work knowing their children were safe

- local delivery services who went out every day to ensure people had the products, prescriptions, post and other personal essentials they needed
- public transport drivers that made it possible for essential workers to get to work each day so they could protect us all

Fast forward two years and the global pandemic had an impact no one in the global community could have imagined.

EARLY LEADERSHIP LEARNINGS

In the early, turbulent times of COVID-19, there was only one thing we knew for sure: we were living in times of profound uncertainty. Whatever the pandemic had in store for us, we were always going to be looking at a future very different from our past.

People would say repeatedly that they wanted to go back to normal. But there was no going back. And there certainly was no normal. Everything we knew to be normal – the way we lived, worked, learned, played, loved and cared for one another, and especially the way in which we viewed the future – was being shifted. For the first time in our generation and as a global community, our world had stopped.

The only way to look to the future was in the short term, understanding how to work through the next normal. This is where the first signs of leadership began to emerge as certain individuals endeavoured to identify and navigate their way into the eye of the storm, in order to gain some sense of control, even if that only meant for small windows of time and within small spheres of influence.

CHAPTER 3

GROUNDED: GLOBAL TRAVEL GOING NOWHERE

I think the moments during the early stages of the pandemic, where it really illustrated how difficult this was, was in May 2020 when during the entire month of May, the same number of passengers passed through DXB as had passed through in only four hours in May 2019.

PAUL GRIFFITHS, CEO, DUBAI INTERNATIONAL AIRPORT (DAA)

So why does this book focus on the travel and tourism industry? Because we have never felt the impact on our inability to travel as strongly as we did during the global pandemic, when we were all grounded. At that time, we understood how essential travel is for literally a billion-plus travellers across the world. It is a source of definition, inspiration, passion, vocation, opportunity and mobilisation. We can all relate to the beauty, business and blessing that travel brings to our lives, both personally and professionally. It is a truth we all know in our hearts.

And importantly, it is what *I know*. Working in the travel and tourism sector has been my profession, and calling, for over two decades. The sector's ability to transform lives, livelihoods, landscapes and legacies for the better, for generations to come, remains the heartbeat of my commitment to what is a truly remarkable global industry and professional community.

Why? Because travel and tourism taps into so many human truths, especially this:

> *We all need to connect with others.*
> *We all need care, compassion and companionship.*
> *We need the ever-changing stimulus of sound, sight*
> *and scent. We need space to breathe, to think,*
> *to dream, and importantly, to decompress.*
> *We need to get out. We need to travel.*

And the places we travel to need us to keep their residents strong, proudly productive, globally connected and hopeful for the future. This I know to be true.

Travel and tourism is also about *who* I know. At a time when our global industry and community could not go anywhere, I observed exceptional leadership in the travel and tourism industry, leaders who were focused, fearless and tireless.

GOVERNMENT PRIORITY #1

As shared earlier, the highly infectious nature of this pandemic meant that not only were we at risk of suffering the often-fatal impact of the virus, but we were also at risk of passing it on to those we loved. And so, putting the health of citizens as priority #1, governments abruptly closed borders. For extended periods of time, for many good reasons, the world was grounded.

Being grounded for the first time in our lifetimes, forced to stay apart from people across the office hallway, across the street and across the world, made it abundantly clear that the psychological impact of physical lockdowns was causing a growing mental-health crisis. This is exactly why the shutdown of the global travel and tourism industry had an impact far beyond those working in the industry themselves. It was not just about the travel ecosystem – airlines, airports, cruise ships, railways, hotels and resorts, attractions, destination marketing entities, the travel trade, and every other link in the travel experience chain – it was about us, the travellers across the globe. With so many extreme measures being put in place regarding any human movement beyond the four walls of their homes, anyone in the world seeking to travel was thrown into a state of severe confusion, frustration and often desperation. Not to mention severe disappointment.

Please just think about it for a moment. We all know how sweet the anticipation of being with someone, somewhere can be. We also all know that while travel across the world is a gift that we all have at our disposal, the planning and mobilisation of travel logistics can be complex. Pre-COVID-19 the main concerns were limited to passport validity, visas, currencies, pre-travel timings and e-connectivity. We were used to the requirements. We knew the travel routine. Naturally we all had questions and concerns that arose alongside the spread of the virus, such as:

What if airlines cancel flights? Or go bankrupt?

What if borders suddenly close?

What if quarantine regulations change, forcing travellers to pay to stay in both time and money?

What if we catch COVID-19 while travelling?

Even when restrictions eased, the cautious response of travellers was understandable:

What if the restrictions change again, for the worse?

What if we get stopped at the border because of incorrect documentation?

What if we suddenly need to cancel and lose our holiday money?

After experiencing the impact of the virus on our daily lives and repeatedly having to cancel or postpone long-awaited travel plans due to the pandemic, it's natural that many of us had these concerns. As travellers, we asked ourselves and others valid questions, including: Why am I bothering?

The trauma of the pandemic in the travel and tourism industry was magnified. With such uncertainty, we were forced to wait it out. But no wait can be without consequence. After a period of time, many small and large businesses, especially small, were forced to step out of the industry they so loved. Why? Because the reality is this: for those in most areas of our industry, there was no remote work-from-home option. You cannot check in non-existent guests to a closed hotel or show off destination highlights to travellers who cannot safely visit. In the early days of the pandemic, the lucky ones had some type of government financial assistance, but for many companies and their employees, this only helped initially. It became too much to sustain with no incoming revenue, zero in many cases, negative in most. Customer interaction turned to refunds.

It is important to remember that less than a hundred days before the declaration of a global pandemic, the travel and tourism sector was growing faster annually than any other sector in the world. We were all so proud and so confident. Over 1.5 billion international arrivals had occurred in 2019. That meant that over four million people were crossing international borders every day. Hopes, hugs, handshakes, dreams, opportunities and possibilities were venturing out across the globe. The aviation industry alone recorded over thirty-eight million flights in 2019.

The global travel industry brought excitement to travellers and had a significant economic impact, accounting for over 10% of global GDP ($9.6 trillion) and generating $1.8 trillion in international visitor spending (6.8% of total exports). Also, the industry is credited for one out of every ten jobs worldwide (333 million). And these jobs were not just any jobs, they were fulfilling careers that allowed people to travel the world, meet new people, explore new places, learn new languages, acquire new skills, experience different cultures and indulge in fantastic global cuisine. It was a joy to work in this industry because every moment and every air mile was filled with love and excitement.

We loved it, every moment, every air mile, every memory.

For especially young people, extroverts, entrepreneurs and executives with itchy feet, travel and tourism (which includes hospitality) was such a fabulous, envied, inspiring industry. It was an industry that offered potential beyond borders and beyond one's wildest dreams because it offered a lifestyle of working beyond the usual. But by the end of 2020, we saw and felt COVID-19 bringing the industry to its knees with shutdowns resulting in losses of over one million jobs per day. Which meant for millions upon millions of students, small businesses, speciality services and even staff of large global corporations with brands that have been around for a lifetime, this was the end of the line.

Leaders saw it happening. They knew the gravity of the situation. They knew the hard decisions that were going to have to be made. The devastation to the industry was visible. The anxiety was palpable. Even if they could hold on a little longer, the cost of reopening, even to local visitors, was mounting. Take the hotel industry as an example: on top of regulations insisting guests were socially distanced and able to utilise only specifically defined parts of the property, thereby severely reducing capacity, costly sanitation, cleaning and protective equipment became an imperative for keeping the doors open and for travellers' peace of mind. And then there was the even bigger issue: the staff to work the desks and clean the rooms.

At some point during the endless time of the pandemic, leaders found they simply could not afford to wait any longer. Changes needed to happen quickly, to stop the bleeding. Some changes were operational, aggressively so. For many business owners and their employees, they had to make the call: they were done. These were people, entities, legacies we knew and worked alongside. We watched so many of them suffer losses greater than they could ever have planned for, and that still cannot be comprehended.

In the first year of the pandemic alone, we experienced a shock like no other in the history of the industry, one that yanked us all back thirty years to levels of travel and tourism activity seen in the early 1990s when nations were guarded, growth was slow, and global discovery was not a priority. Is this too dramatic a statement? Not at all. To put this into perspective, the pandemic was pushing us back to a time before Google, a time when the Berlin Wall had just come down, Cold War tensions were yet to subside, and the euro was still almost a decade away from being introduced. It can feel hard to imagine those times, as in the three decades that followed the global travel sector had flourished with technology fuelling the ability of travel dreams to turn quickly and confidently into bookings. We all lived it − we all loved it! Which is why the final 2020 statistics express a story that today can feel beyond fiction. And yet it was painfully real. As reported by the United Nations World Tourism Organization (UNWTO) in their November 2021 publication, *The Economic Contribution of Tourism and the Impact of COVID-19*:

> *Tourism suffered the greatest crisis on record in 2020 following an unprecedented health, social and economic emergency with the outbreak of the COVID-19 pandemic.*
>
> *International tourist arrivals (overnight visitors) plunged by 73% in 2020 due to a global lockdown, widespread travel restrictions and a massive drop in demand. About 1 billion fewer international arrivals were recorded that year compared to 2019, $1.3 trillion dollars in international tourism receipt losses.*
>
> *The COVID-19 pandemic was responsible for about 70% of the world's loss of GDP in 2020, which amounted to $2.8 trillion.*

I recall vividly early in the crisis the first time the UNWTO reported estimated losses for 2020 vs. 2019 to be greater than 60% (the final number for 2020 was 74%). I sat quietly in my office staring at the screen, pausing all other endless activity I was immersed in to help keep clients and colleagues' hopes buoyant. And I cried. Seeing this information officially published was agonising because it made it real.

As frightening as the tourism activity stats was traveller sentiment. Fear was growing as the virus was spreading. Even if people could travel, no one had any interest in going. The risks were just too high, the consequences too scary.

Thankfully, in parallel with the race to stop the spread, scale and severity of the healthcare crisis that gripped the world, a race was taking place within the medical community. Its aim: find a vaccine to tame the beast that was COVID-19.

Never before had the global medical community worked so intensely, so rapidly and in collaboration to create, clinically trial, gain approval for, manufacture, distribute and ultimately administer the tiny little glass vials that would reduce the severity of impact of the virus and help reduce the fear. And then it happened: at the end of 2020 came an official announcement from the WHO and CDC that offered a real ray of hope for people across the globe, and a way of unlocking global borders and skies: approval of a vaccine. Not a vaccine to cure COVID-19 – that was too tall a task in too short a time, especially noting the 'novel', never known before nature of the virus. This was a vaccine that would mitigate the risk of us getting severely ill or dying from COVID-19. During December 2020, one year from the first global whispers of a fatal, highly transmittable, previously unknown virus being detected in China, the first doses of the vaccine began to be administered.

Global leaders took to the front line of the quest for global vaccination, stepping into action like never seen before. It was one of those rare times when the need to win as a global community eclipsed the desire for individual entities and societies to outdo others. Competitors became co-creators; the greatest minds and methods being applied towards the greatest healthcare race of our generation.

The global travel and tourism community was part of this show of force, an invaluable part of the race for global safety. Especially leaders within the aviation industry, hearing the call of duty they became the new frontliners. The industry transformed into a global vaccine distribution task force. Cargo airlines opened their holds to load thousands of containers of vaccines destined for nations across the globe while commercial aircraft were stripped of their seating to further elevate vaccine reach, loading pallets where passengers once sat, doing whatever it took to mobilise global access to vaccination. DHL estimated that the global distribution of vaccines and accompanying cooler boxes would require over 15,000 chilled cargo flights over the 2021 and 2022 period, according to an article by a law firm.[4]

(SOURCE: NEWSPAPER HEADLINES, UNSPLASH)

Please bear in mind that these leaders of the aviation community took on this humanitarian call of duty having endured almost a year of grounding. If any industry could not afford to take on additional expenses it was aviation. But these leaders knew that they could not afford to *not* act. The calling was clear.

The time was now. And so they did – they acted with speed and scale. This show of leadership, individually and collectively, remains one of the greatest shows of force, unity and hope during those exceptionally demanding times.

(SOURCES TOP/LEFT TO RIGHT: PHOTO BY LUKAS SOUZA FROM UNSPLASH. CANVA PRO LICENSE, NO ATTRIBUTION REQUIRED. SUVARNABHUMI AIRPORT (BKK), 17 MAY 2020, PHOTO BY AIYTAN FROM UNSPLASH)

For the next two years acute focus was applied to the global distribution and administration of approved vaccines, and to global networks working to ensure equitable production, distribution, administration, and eventually re-vaccination (including boosters). With vaccinations came confidence in our world being able to reopen to travel.

By 2021, the restrictions and lockdowns began to shift geographically. More countries slowly, cautiously, though sadly inconsistently, started to ease wide-scale restrictions. Being able to travel locally (domestic tourism) offered glimmers of hope for recovery, with the WTTC reporting that 88.3% of tourists chose to travel within a radius of 186 miles (300 km) of their homes in 2021. Hotel bookings in Europe jumped 200% in 2021 compared to 2019, according to the online booking site Trip.com, as travellers embraced staycations and the upsides to new work-from-anywhere lifestyles.

Sadly, we soon saw that the vaccine roll-out was accompanied by a roll-out of political ideologies that separated nations, breaking the unity of the global community that ironically the virus inspired. The masked versus the non-masked and finally the vaccinated versus the non-vaccinated. This was an important shift, as travel and tourism became stuck in the middle of government regulations versus required mandates of travel versus traveller sentiment. It was heartbreaking to see families, friends, colleagues and strangers becoming divided when we all needed to remain united in this war against the virus.

Slowly, very slowly, borders began to open in some areas of the world. But when international borders reopened there was a price to pay. For some it meant testing for coronavirus, vaccine passports, or quarantine hotels, for others it meant finding themselves stuck in destinations when restrictions changed in an instant. For the airline industry, hotels and online booking agents, customer safety and security became their assumed responsibility, despite having little influence on the crisis itself. How could this be? Our world had come so far, together.

By 2022, travel began to get easier yet again. Restrictions became more streamlined in most areas of the world or they were scrapped altogether. Airbnb, Booking.com, TripAdvisor and Expedia showed that the most popular destinations recovered to around pre-pandemic levels, with the highest increase recorded in February and May, up 10.9% and 5.6% respectively compared to 2019. With 2022 bookings surpassing

NHS **COVID Pass Travel**

DOSE
2

NAME
ANITA MENDIRATTA

DATE OF BIRTH
17 June 1968

BARCODE VALID UNTIL
23 October 2021

PRODUCT
Vaxzevria

DATE OF DOSE 2
12 June 2021

(SOURCE: ANITA MENDIRATTA)

pre-pandemic levels, the recovery of our industry was finally in sight. But there was one major hurdle left: serious staffing shortages right across the travel and tourism ecosystem and traveller experience chain. According to the economic impact report of 2021 by WTTC, the number of jobs supported by travel and tourism experienced a significant decline of 18.6% from 2019 to 2020, from 333 million jobs to 271 million. The workforce needed to support real recovery was no longer there. At the time of writing this book, the shortfalls in securing consistent, qualified staff remain.

(SOURCE: YOUNG MAN UPSET AFTER FLIGHT CANCELLATION, ADOBE STOCK. STAFF WANTED NOTICE IN DUBLIN, IRELAND IN 2022, HELPSTAY, UNSPLASH. LARGE AMOUNT OF LOST BAGGAGE AT THE AIRPORT, 2022, ANTON GVOZDIKOV.)

As mentioned earlier, so many people working in the industry, across the travel experience chain, were simply forced to leave the industry. They needed to find a way to survive. They needed to find a way to make money immediately. They could not wait for later, there was no sense of how long it would take for later to arrive. In many ways, it is so understandable. During the global pandemic, it was the young people who suffered deeply at a personal level and they were mainly the service staff in hotels, restaurants, resorts and attractions, airports, airlines, special events and all the other frontline roles. Stuck at home with reduced hours, reduced pay and reduced hope, they found new ways to not only become productive in the new work-from-anywhere environment, but also found a way of working with purpose. And many industries were very happy to take them on board, as they recognised the exceptional emotional intelligence that these hospitality and travel industry service-skilled young people possessed.

By the autumn of 2022, bookings were up, travellers were feeling confident again. But the staffing shortages remained and the industry continues to face unique challenges in trying to fully recover, as global travel engines continue to groan out of their induced coma to re-establish pre-pandemic levels of a global movement of people and products to, from and within places across the world.

ONE CRISIS LEADS INTO ANOTHER

It's important to acknowledge that the pandemic was not the only crisis we faced in 2020, nor is its recovery our sole priority. Even prior to the emergence of COVID-19, there were significant challenges to global safety, stability, unity and potential for the future. At a local level, certain parts of the world were already busy working through other crises. Political tensions, perilous weather events, protests unseen before in our generation and highly infectious parasites were already causing havoc when COVID-19 hit.

As shared by Brad Dean of Discover Puerto Rico:

> *You know, we were coming out of a crisis. So, we had just barely reached the point of recovery from a devastating hurricane. And then in Puerto Rico, our 2020 started with three straight weeks of almost daily earthquakes. So, we had just been in crisis and recovery mode for the better part of two and a half years.*

(SOURCES LEFT TO RIGHT: PRIME MINISTER THERESA MAY IS VOTED OUT, THOMAS CHARTERS, UNSPLASH. BREXIT PROTESTS IN LONDON, ENGLAND, LUDOVIC MORLAT, UNSPLASH. ZIKA VIRUS SETS GLOBAL ALARM, MCCAIG. HURRICANE DORIAN HITS NORTHERN BAHAMAS. SHUBHAM SINGH, GETTY IMAGES. MASS PROTESTS IN HONG KONG, MANSON YIM, UNSPLASH.)

Part of me recognised that this was just going to launch us into a whole new level of uncertainty, but there was also a sense of resilience that, 'Hey, we've got this'. At least that's what I was trying to convey. We've been through earthquakes, we've been through hurricanes, we've been through financial bankruptcy for the whole island. We're going to handle this. And if you recall back in around 2015–16, Puerto Rico had experienced the Zika virus. So there at least had been some thought put into our crisis recovery plan about communicable diseases.

> *Of course, none of us were prepared for what COVID-19 was going to deliver, but we at least went into it feeling like we had our bearings on how to handle a crisis.*

The year 2021 was also not without incident beyond COVID-19. The world struggled with crisis after crisis that brought layer after layer of immense local, regional and global disruption. From civil rights and political protests to previously unseen mega-infrastructure catastrophes and extreme weather disasters, direct and often violent challenges to global security and connectivity added to the already extreme instability caused by the pandemic.

By the end of 2022, in addition to the global health, economic and social trauma caused by two years of the pandemic, the year closed with the world facing the following challenges:

- Economic:
  - energy crisis
  - rising interest rates
  - supply chain disruptions
  - manufacturing reductions
  - fears of global recession
  - unemployment
- Political:
  - Russia's invasion of Ukraine
  - populism
  - citizenry uprisings
- Environmental:
  - ongoing climate crisis
  - severe weather conditions
- Social:
  - inequality
  - lack of diversity
  - elevated poverty
  - migration
  - human slavery

(SOURCES: PORT OF BEIRUT EXPLOSION, PHOTO TAKEN DAYS AFTER THE EXPLOSION FROM AN ADJACENT BUILDING. RASHID HREISS, UNSPLASH. NEWSPAPER ON 7 JANUARY 2021 IN HONOLULU, HAWAII. LITTLE PLANT, UNSPLASH. FOREST FIRE, MIKHAIL SERDYUKOV, UNSPLASH. STOP KILLING AFGHAN PROTEST IN LONDON, EHIMETALOR AKHERE UNUABONA, UNSPLASH.)

These crises all ran parallel to the lingering, deeply disturbing and debilitating after-effects of COVID-19, including long COVID and the mental health crisis. The challenges continue to put immense pressure on global governments, societies, communities, environments and opportunities. They test the strength of a term that became an omnipresent, often overused part of the COVID-19 vernacular: resilience. These challenges will continue to exert pressure on the global travel and tourism industry, testing its resilience. However, the industry has proven time and again, including during the pandemic and in previous crises, that it is an enduring and remarkable example of resilience that the world can rely on. And thankfully so, because we know the impact of travel and tourism goes far, far beyond our industry.

WHY DOES TRAVEL AND TOURISM REALLY MATTER?

Let's rewind to the beginning of the twenty-first century to get an aerial perspective on the travel and tourism industry. Just over two decades ago, there was an awakening that changed how nations connected at all levels. It caused seismic shifts in the social, economic, cultural and political makeup of the world we now live in. And yet it is so easy to forget just what was happening in the world at that time. So, what was happening? Let's look closely at the macro forces of change.

First, it was a time of the rise of emerging markets – a time also referred to as 'the rise of the many'. Technically speaking, an emerging market is a 'developing' nation that is working to elevate itself to 'developed' status as defined by the World Bank Group and the International Monetary Fund (IMF). Their focus is on advancing their policies, processes and structures, economically, socially and politically, to put in place solid pillars critical to national growth and development. These countries typically have less developed capital markets, lower levels of per capita income and need to significantly establish (and therefore invest in) the core infrastructure needed for high levels of participation and productivity in the local economy, as well as global connectivity. This means they need to significantly elevate the ability for their people, industry and institutions to work together within the country, as well as with the global economy. And they need to create meaning for these extraordinary efforts.

The early twenty-first century saw a number of countries once deemed 'developing' that were rich in resources, had high populations and high aspirations, rise up as active, aspirational members of the global market community. In 2001 Brazil, Russia, India and China, the simply termed BRIC nations, led the way, providing a united, inspiring example of what was possible for nations seeking to become more significant on the global landscape and on the global competitive field. Together they represented over 2.6 billion citizens, a breath-taking 43% of the world's population at the time. In 2010, South Africa joined the community, creating BRICS and adding over fifty million citizens to the high-rising cluster. Just imagine the impact that number of economically empowered people can have on how the world connects, creates, makes choices, spends, invests and moves! Unsurprisingly, they shifted the centre of global growth, productivity and spending power towards the East.

Globalisation led companies to explore new markets, partnerships, processes and business methods, resulting in the reshaping of global market activity and the flow of money, which in turn fuelled growth both individually and symbiotically. A central factor at this time of exceptional growth and confidence was the emergence of two forces that in many ways dissolved borders between nations:

- the growth of the e-connection and e-commerce as a result of huge advances in the internet and digital technology
- the growth of the services sector, enabling citizens to play a more active, engaged, globally exposed role in their economy and society

With the world opening up, travel and tourism became a natural runway for the global community to redefine the future and what they wanted from it. The massive growth in curiosity and activity resulted in step changes in the industry's ability to operate and benefit; these included the:

- growth of air routes and low-cost carriers significantly reducing costs of travel
- growth in digital marketing and promotion in travel, opening hopeful travellers up to a world of choice in terms of possibility and pricing
- growth in government appreciation of travel and tourism as a primary lever for strengthening national employment, inclusivity, earnings, investment attraction, identity and competitiveness

Governments understood the fact that travel and tourism were getting nations working and building futures. Once viewed as an industry based on play, pleasure and passionate patriotism, the sector finally established a profile of respect and credibility, and as a powerful driver of the economic engine. Countries joining the global tourism sector soon recognised their efforts as a labour of love – a love of country, identity and possibility. Why? Because travel and tourism is in many ways the gift wrapping of a destination, showcasing the destination's most stylish, compelling and inspiring aspects and putting forward a confident, caring invitation to travellers to visit for work and/or play. The act of marketing a nation's natural beauty, its history, lifestyle, culture and the spirit and hospitality of its people enables governments of even small, newly established countries to claim a place on the international tourism map for themselves.

> *By welcoming visitors, the visited can play a part in the growth and development of the place they call 'home'. Each and every individual has the ability to touch, and be touched by, tourism.*

HOW TOURISM IS SHAPING THE FUTURE OF NATIONS

There are four ways travel and tourism work symbiotically to shape the future of nations.

ECONOMICALLY

The travel and tourism industry not only brings in substantial revenues for destinations, but it also has the ability to attract significant investment. These funds can be used to develop infrastructure vital to the growth of the tourism sector, as well as general infrastructure that benefits the local population. Investments can go towards building mass transport systems, airports, networks for Information and Communications Technology (ICT), safety and security services, sports and leisure facilities, hotels and attractions. All of these areas of development are critical for improving the competitiveness of the travel and tourism sector.

POLITICALLY

Travel and tourism is a valuable driver to strengthen the focus, fabric and future advancement of nations. Governments across the globe have recognised the importance of the sector in the unification and development of the economic and social dimensions of nations. In defining the travel and tourism sector as a priority, leaders begin the process of shaping the identity and core objectives for growth.

SOCIALLY

Flowing directly from the above, the travel and tourism sector has proven to be invaluable in bringing people together around a shared national identity and an invitation to the world, regardless of age, race, religion, profession, personality and political point of view. The low barriers of entry to the sector make it possible for all people to play a role in the tourism community and economy, be they artisans, architects, advertisers, travel agents, or government advisors. Everyone has a valuable part to play to ensure that the destination works to deliver a unique, compelling and competitive tourism experience that will sustainably attract visitors for business or leisure travel purposes. And importantly, as tourism experiences are delivered primarily through SMEs (small and medium enterprises), parts of society in emerging nations that were previously unable to join the workforce may contribute through their skills and initiative. As a result, the sector empowers more and more citizens to play a meaningful, recognised role in national growth and upliftment.

PSYCHOLOGICALLY

Travel is no longer about logistical movement from A to B. It is about social movement, economic movement, spiritual movement and the movement of cultures closer to one another. Travel has become a vehicle for showing oneself, and others. And when it comes to business, it has become essential in breaking down barriers and out-of-date perceptions about who we used to be. In addition to playing a part in one's individual identity, travel has become a form of personal therapy through the opportunity to escape, experience, exhale, whatever the need may be in these increasingly stressful times.

Tourism provides countries with a platform for wealth creation and nation building. Governments are reassured that their people are working together towards a more prosperous, promising future for themselves and their families, built on a solid past and sense of the present. The joy of travel is also felt by the people who proudly share their special part of the world with visitors, knowing they are playing an important role in the growth and development of their home through tourism.

Leaders in the industry have always been acutely aware of the fact that travel is the ultimate form of diplomacy – it is soft power at its best. That said, by 2020 leaders across the industry were recognising that their skills were vital to ensuring that the industry maintained its position of being a force for good. Their leadership inspired investment, visits, innovation and collaboration while carefully managing the speed, scope and scale of impact at a local level, especially socially, culturally and environmentally.

Little did these same leaders know how their leadership was about to be tested.

CHAPTER 4

UNDERSTANDING OUR WIRING:
HOW OUR BRAINS WORK DURING CRISIS

You can't confront fear with power.

JULIA SIMPSON, PRESIDENT AND CEO, WORLD TRAVEL & TOURISM COUNCIL (WTTC)

Dealing with a crisis is not new to us. It has happened before, and we know it will happen again. Sometimes it happens to us, at other times, it happens around us. Sometimes a crisis is personal, other times it is professional. It may be external: an extreme weather event, an economic shock, an act of God, or an act of angry men. Whatever the case, a crisis challenges us and it changes us. You, me, none of us are immune.

A crisis, by definition, refers to a period marked by imminent danger, difficulty, or uncertainty that necessitates problem-solving and crucial decision-making. By implication, it is a shock to our system that has such an impact on our sense of safety, stability and security that it puts us into a raw state of emotion and physiological reaction. Our wiring puts our minds into action, mobilising our bodies, setting us on a path that we hope, and pray, will yield a positive outcome.

As much as we can hope we are always ready when a crisis occurs, these moments strike without warning, without consideration, and without compassion. They force us to make some of the most important decisions of our lives within a split second.

It is safe to say that we have all made decisions that have left us feeling safe, secure and thankful. Reflecting on our actions, we gain a new confidence in our ability to instinctively respond as needed to get to the other side. We are quietly proud of what we have seen in ourselves. On the other hand, there will be those decisions that leave us disappointed in ourselves. We let ourselves, and sadly others, down. All these thoughts, actions and reactions reinforce our wiring – how our minds process situations and then proceed to make decisions that, as we have seen, may leave us either proud of who we are or pained by how we could have been more.

In so many ways, the crises we endure in life become defining features of who we are. Like scars, they create undeniable imprints, even if no scars are visible on our bodies. We can try so hard to avoid looking at or thinking of them, but then something apparently simple becomes a trigger, poking at the scar, unlocking the pain within. These triggers are directly connected to memories, which are connected to moments tied to a crisis. This crisis is now connected to us.

Triggers have a terrible way of sneaking up on us. Time does not weaken them, nor does distance. Years may go by and then suddenly it happens. You hear a sound: a specific piece of music, a passing siren, a distinctive person's voice, a painful child's cry. Or maybe it is recognising a scent: a gentle puff of smoke, a sharp whiff of antibacterial liquid, a hint of jasmine in the air. These triggers can take us right back to the crisis, locking our thoughts and impacting our actions. One's wiring feels blocked, barred from being able to move forward and free oneself from the past.

For some, however, understanding the triggers becomes a way of resetting their wiring, breaking the blockages, and enabling the flow. It's all about our wiring – one of the most fundamental aspects of who we are in the best of times, and especially in the worst. Therefore, writing a book on how leaders responded in times of crisis without going into the basics of how the brain and body respond in moments of crisis would not only be incomplete, but it would also be irresponsible.

Understanding and respecting the minds of leaders in this book and how they responded when our most recent global crisis occurred, is central to learn from their decisions and actions. We need to understand how these leaders took control of their own physiological and emotional responses, making the most of their wiring.

That said, I'm not a technical expert on the workings of the brain, nor am I a psychiatrist or psychologist. I cannot take the science and marry it to years of research and study that exists across the global medical community. I am a travel and tourism practitioner with immense respect for the world of intelligence that we need to tap into in order to learn how we can access and adjust our wiring to help us become stronger when we next face a crisis.

What are the important things we need to know about the human brain and its response during and after a crisis? Thankfully, enormous amounts of scientific study have already been conducted into understanding both the immediate and long-lasting impact of trauma.

But where did the word trauma come from? Weren't we focusing on crisis? Yes, so let's pause for a moment and look more closely at what I mean when referring to crisis compared to trauma. Crisis can be defined as an extremely upsetting or dangerous situation. Trauma can be defined as severe and lasting emotional shock and pain caused by an extremely upsetting experience. It is safe to say that trauma is often an *after-effect* of a crisis. Wiring is, therefore, how trauma is internalised and embedded into the mind, consciously and subconsciously.

Few get through trauma unscathed. Few get through unhaunted and/ or undaunted. Images and echoes linger for years, as memories, memorials and milestones keep the sense of loss alive. We know this is a painful after-effect of trauma. After the pandemic, the sight of face masks, the smell of hand sanitiser may become triggers reconnecting us to the fact that we lived through a time that now seems like fiction; we did struggle, we did survive, but at the same time, we did suffer. These triggers are especially jarring because they can sneak up on us. Without warning, music, images, scents and sounds suddenly reawaken reflections and recollections in ways that take one back, regardless of how much time has passed or how much healing has occurred. But there is hope, as the leaders profiled in this book reveal.

If we can help individuals incorporate the impact of a crisis into their cognitive wiring, it can enhance their ability to process information, manage their fear and take appropriate action when another crisis arises. This rewiring can become their superpower, enabling them to weather the storm and emerge stronger in the aftermath. Reflections on times of crisis may become a source of pride, proof of possibility, a way of understanding oneself for the better. Triggers may become a source of fuel for the mind and heart, consciously and/or subconsciously providing energy and focus, and a way of reconnecting people with their sense of purpose. As many leaders who have bravely led through crises have testified, it is in these moments when they feel most alive.

What causes us to respond to events in different ways? We often call it our gut instinct – we just did it. Our response was as simple and basic as that. Sometimes it worked out: sometimes it did not. It's just how we are wired. There is, however, no *just* about it. And there is no need to feel at the mercy of our wiring. It is a sincere hope that this book will use its own careful, respectful study of the leaders profiled to establish themes of understanding that help us all recognise and work with the wiring we have within us.

> *By better understanding our wiring, and therefore ourselves, we have the potential to face future challenges with greater self-awareness, self-appreciation, and even self-care.*

THE BASICS OF THE BRAIN AND THE IMPORTANCE OF FEAR

Dr Sanjay Gupta, one of the invaluable contributors to this book who is not only CNN's Chief Medical Correspondent but also a brilliant practising neurosurgeon, beautifully describes in his book *World War C* the power station that is the human brain when he says:

> *The human brain is a remarkable organ, an evolutionary marvel. Scientists often describe it as the most complex thing we have ever discovered: one of the discoverers of DNA went so far as to call it 'the last and grandest biological frontier'. It is arguably the most enigmatic 3.3 pounds of tissue in our universe.*

The awe of the power of the brain's wiring is elevated when one thinks of how leaders are able to look fear in the eye, their wiring responding in a way that unlocks clarity, confidence and courage.

To learn from their example, what is important for us to know about how the brain responds to a crisis? How can we not only comprehend what happens to us but also take control to minimise the damage? And how can we better understand and potentially rewire our cognitive processes to help us navigate the storm? It all starts with understanding our individual relationship with fear. The human body is diversely and vastly interconnected. As expressed on the WHO website:

The brain is arguably the most complex organ in the human body and recognised as the body's command centre, influencing every aspect of life. Brain health is the state of brain functioning across cognitive, sensory, social-emotional, behavioural and motor domains, allowing a person to realise their full potential over the life course. Numerous interconnected determinants pertaining to physical health, healthy environments, safety, and security, learning and social connection as well as access to quality services influence the way our brains develop, adapt and respond to stress and adversity.

Fear is the biochemical and emotional response when sensing danger. It is a natural part of the human experience, personal development and ultimately survival. Fear also plays an important part when it comes to our ability to recognise and respond in a crisis, and whether or not our response seeds trauma.

Fear triggers a number of responses in the mind and body that are best described by three universally accepted elements when we perceive a threat to our safety: fight, flight or freeze. This concept is not new and has become so ingrained in human development that it's now woven into the fabric of our understanding. But where did the concept come from, and when?

The origins of fight, flight or freeze go back to the early 1900s when American physiologist Walter Bradford Cannon studied animals' responses to stress and danger. When faced with a threat, animals would either fight back, run away, or freeze in place. These responses were a natural and instinctive way for them to protect themselves from harm. Later, the concept was further developed by psychologist Walter Hess and psychiatrist Hans Selye, who focused on the physiological changes that occur in the body during a stress response. They observed that the fight, flight or freeze response involves the activation of the sympathetic nervous system and the release of stress hormones, such as adrenaline and cortisol. Today, these findings are widely used by psychologists to help people understand and manage their stress and anxiety responses.

The fight, flight or freeze response is a fundamental aspect of our survival because it helps us recognise when we are experiencing stress or anxiety and can give us an insight into why we may be feeling this way. This applies to many different contexts, such as in the workplace, in personal relationships, and in dealing with traumatic events. By understanding how we react to stress, we can take steps to manage our responses and prevent negative consequences.

The response most frequently spotlighted in times of crisis is: fight. When a threat is sensed this response motivates and helps us instinctively take action to protect ourselves, and others if needed. It unlocks an instinctive effort to confront, resist, or simply get through a moment of challenge. Taking control during a crisis means taking action to navigate through it. This includes mobilising ideas, people and resources to face the challenge, making plans to emerge stronger, and even addressing underlying issues that may have led to the crisis in the first place. The fight response is all about not sitting still and waiting for the crisis to define the outcome. This type of response is known to carry significant risk, as individuals willingly put themselves in harm's way. However, their wiring has adapted to accept this behaviour. When they smell smoke, they run towards what they know could be a fire. This courage is applauded – this is how heroes emerge like a phoenix rising from the flames.

And then there is flight. In this response, the priority is to immediately remove oneself from harm's way. Smelling smoke, people instinctively run away to avoid the possible danger of a fire, or even the chance of experiencing it again. Sadly, flight is often viewed as a weaker response compared to fight, as it is seen as a lack of confidence in overcoming the challenge, or even a fear of failure. It is not always a physical response, it can also be emotional, such as backing away from a difficult conversation or a hard decision. Sadly, any flight situation leaves unfinished business as regret may follow, opportunities may be missed, and a quick escape may leave damage behind.

Finally, there is the freeze response. It is when a fear of the unknown, or a fear of uncertainty, becomes so debilitating that we are unable to react at all and become paralysed by our own thoughts. If we smell smoke, we do not know which way to turn. We have all had that experience at some point in our lives, even if only for a mere moment. The reaction is a simple survival mechanism that most often happens with external emergencies: a response to a personal attack or being hit by extreme weather. Why do we freeze? To give our brain a moment to figure out what is happening and what is next. The duration of the freeze is the issue. As with the flight response, the longer the freeze, the greater the risk of regret and even greater damage occurring.

Typically, discussions around the response to fear are based on short-term sensations of risk. These risks may be an immediate sense of physical unsafety, such as walking home late at night on a poorly lit street; feeling uncomfortable in an elevator with strangers; becoming unnerved by the increasing growl of a dog; realising a break-in has occurred at home; or even simply feeling watched. Or the risk may be an emotional fear based on a short-term shock, such as hearing about the loss of a job; the break-up of a relationship; or a medical diagnosis that is life-threatening.

The immediate response to fear has a distinct physiological reaction. The stress being experienced, the adrenaline released, and the surge of the brain's alertness all work to heighten the awareness of risk, and ability to act.

> *In a moment of perceived risk, the feelings are real, and they are consuming. Importantly, these feelings embed themselves into the wiring we store in our minds and bodies linked to how we recognised and responded to fear at that moment and then for the rest of our lives.*

Never before have we as a global community had to face wave after wave after wave of crisis as virus mutations, spreads and reinfections triggered one period of limitations on our lives after another. Even as time passed and we became more used to living with the pandemic, we felt the strain, both physically and mentally, and we faced the risk of reinfection.

This was an important aspect of our shared crisis. In the early days of 2020, when we thought we were at the highest risk of becoming infected by an out-of-control virus, the signature sights, sounds, scents and other fear-provoking sensations became deeply embedded in our minds and hearts. From our respective lockdowns, viewing the world through our television, tablet, mobile phone, or other screens, our world seemed to become an army of medical workers in blue PPE (personal protective equipment), only distinguishable by their eyes and ID badges. News coverage across the globe looked the same:

- The horrifying sight of people of all ages lying in row after row of hospital beds, all hooked up to respirators, all desperately trying to breathe, while exhausted nurses working 24/7 checked their vital signs, hoping the fear in their eyes would not be seen by a visibly terrified patient.
- Medical teams scrambling to find more oxygen to help the hundreds of people lined up on the streets seeking care, their bodies collapsing from the fear and fatigue.
- Makeshift morgues filling up at an alarming speed with body bags big and small of those who had no chance of fighting whatever this thing was that was taking over their systems.
- City skies turning a deadly shade of grey with smoke as flames rose high above lines of funeral pyres cremating more and more of those who lost their lives, with the tears of onlooking mourners flowing.
- Families crowded around computer screens to say their final words to a dying loved one they are unable to visit or hold one last time, as the cold touch of a tablet in the hands of a hospital caregiver is the only way for the dying person to see those they so adore before closing their eyes for the last time.
- A child's tiny hand pressed up against a window hoping to feel even the slightest bit of warmth from their grandparent's hand on the other side.

And then there were our other senses being assaulted as we adjusted to:

- the piercing sound of ambulance sirens on otherwise silent streets
- the scent of hand sanitiser overpowering every fresh space
- the rapid pace of breaking news sharing something new to be afraid of or something we needed to be prepared for
- the clang of metal pans being struck at night as communities gathered in doorways and on balconies to clap for carers

These sights, sounds, scents, and so many other stimuli, along with stories we were hearing from friends, family, colleagues and others within our daily worlds, reinforced a sense of fear, a feeling of profound vulnerability, and an unprecedented level of uncertainty.

The initial hundred days of the first wave of the pandemic were dramatic. We all remember the unique sense of fear that we felt, it was primal. And yet, much as it was terrifying, it was also unifying. Together, we all were forced to face the fear. Together, we had to move forward. Together, we just had to adjust. Together, we held on, absorbing into our systems sustained fear, both psychologically and physically. We were all in this together, even if we felt so very alone.

How was this possible? How exactly does our brain take all the fear in? How does this fear impact how we respond, internally and externally? And what does our wiring have to do with it?

BACK TO THE BASICS OF THE BRAIN

How do we possibly begin to encapsulate the complexities of how our brains work and how they respond in a moment of crisis? It is not an easy task, but a necessary one if we are to:

- honour the gift and power of our grey matter
- understand how sensing a crisis impacts our actions and emotions
- appreciate the actions of those who led us through recent crisis-consumed times

So, let us take this step by step, or rather section by section. The first part of the brain to consider is the amygdala. We all know how a moment of crisis can set our minds racing, with every part of our body feeling electrified because of all the thoughts being sparked. The amygdala plays a vital role as the manager of our emotions. These emotions can either direct or derail our ability to think and act clearly. This almond-shaped structure is responsible for processing emotions that trigger our body's fight, flight or freeze response. The amygdala is the first line of defence in a crisis, and it quickly reacts when danger is sensed by releasing hormones that increase heart rate, blood pressure and breathing rate. Our attention is grabbed, preparing our body to either fight or flee the perceived danger being faced.

Like two hands clapping, the amygdala works with the next part of the brain that is essential in a crisis, the prefrontal cortex. This part of our brain is responsible for decision-making and problem-solving. It helps us make quick decisions by evaluating the situation and choosing the best course of action. In a crisis, the prefrontal cortex is hard at work for us, processing information to establish what actions we need to take to stay safe. Think about the task this part of the brain has, the power, strength and quality of its processing cannot but leave one awed!

(SOURCE: ANITA MENDIRATTA)

None of this just happens without consequences: our wiring is impacted, and memories are made. This is where the next essential part of our crisis response ecosystem lies, in the hippocampus. This is our memory vault, helping us remember what we have learned from past experiences, and recall information from the past that may be useful in our response in the present. This part of the brain is critical in a crisis, especially for the freeze response.

A moment of shock can erase our ability to remember important details, such as phone numbers, names and plans. The hippocampus adds thoughts to our instinctive actions. For example, if the fire alarm goes off when you are asleep in a hotel, the hippocampus will help you to think of exactly what you need to do, right now, quickly. Go and 1) get dressed, 2) grab your passport, room key (in case the smoke forces you to return) and mobile phone, 3) get out!

Our brain's power station in crisis is not limited to these three areas. The thalamus is responsible for gathering information from our senses and sending it to the appropriate part of the brain for processing. In a crisis, the thalamus works hard to relay all the sensory information that comes into the brain, including sights, sounds and sensations both present as well as past. This information, be it in the immediate moment or in memories of times of crisis past, is used to help us make decisions and respond appropriately to a crisis. It is primal, and it is vital to processing information in a crisis.

Another core part of our brain function in a crisis is the brainstem. This part of our brain is responsible for controlling basic functions such as breathing and heart rate. In a crisis, the brainstem works together with the rest of our brain to ensure that our body is functioning properly, especially calming our feeling of over-excitement and keeping focused.

So, what has this quick tour of the brain revealed when it comes to our response to a crisis? We all have five critical parts of the brain working together to keep us functioning when we cannot afford to fall apart. They also help us through to the other side of the chaos.

1. The amygdala: *the processing centre for our emotions*.
2. The prefrontal cortex: *where decision-making happens, working alongside the amygdala.*
3. The hippocampus: *the memory bank, tapping back into information from the past that may be useful in responses now.*
4. The thalamus: *helps to make decisions now by using memories of past incidents with sensory information coming from the brain in the present, to prevent a harmful 'sense, remember, repeat' response cycle.*
5. The brainstem: *our body's internal regulator prevents overzealous over-reaction.*

Remarkably, the entire crisis response happens in a millisecond and is driven by our unconscious brain.

> *We can never predict whether we will choose fight, flight, or freeze in each situation, even if we have been presented with a similar situation in the past.*

We are not, however, at the mercy of the randomness of our responses. When an event occurs that finds us instinctively seeking safety, there is always the opportunity afterwards to look closely and carefully at our responses to understand:

- what exactly it was that we interpreted as a risk
- why and how we reacted emotionally
- how our minds should contextualise the feeling of risk in the future to control our emotional and physical response, especially when it comes to restoring a sense of calm and safety
- how we can get to that state of calm understanding quickly and look beyond the moment of fear and see through to the other side

Here is an example of this process in action. You are standing in a busy, bustling crowd in the middle of one of the world's great tourist cities. The sun is pouring down, the streets are buzzing with cheery travellers, gifted buskers and grateful shopkeepers. As much as it is a strange place, a spot never visited before, it all feels so comforting, welcoming, exciting. Suddenly you hear a loud, cracking pop. And another. And another. Your heart starts to pound. Your eyes widen. You turn in the direction of the sound. Your feet are heavy, yet you feel ready to run from what may have been gunfire. You know about places across the world that have been hit by lone-wolf terrorists trying to make madness happen, somehow making a point. Your wiring readies you for flight, but also reminds you to stop and be certain of the sound's source before racing off and starting to spread panic. Sure enough, a quick look over your shoulder reveals the sound came from champagne corks popping in unison from bottles being cracked open at that charming little café you walked past just minutes ago. Then comes the cheering of the guests celebrating! And the clapping. All is fine, your heart starts to calm. A quiet voice within you whispers 'Relax – it's fine'.

This example shows why insight into how the brain responds to a crisis is so important. It enables us to do two things:

1. understand how we innately, immediately react when we are in a position of perceived risk
2. adjust our reactions to enable us to face future crises in a greater position of calm, control and confidence

That is why this book matters. That is why the response of leaders profiled in this book matters. They clearly demonstrate that their wiring put them into a clear, confident response of fight in a way that was not only helpful and hopeful, but also peaceful. But what difference does this knowledge really make if our wiring is already set? This question forms the core purpose of writing this book. By carefully examining how and why the leaders profiled were able to confidently and courageously step forward we can study and learn from their:

- internalisation of risk
- management of fear
- identification of critical actions
- examples as enduring sources of strength to help us understand how we can guide our own responses in the future, thereby adjusting our wiring

With this in mind (pun unintended), let's look at the fight, flight and freeze responses again in the context of how different leaders in our global travel and tourism community reacted:

- from different parts of the world
- from different areas of the global industry ecosystem
- from different levels of experience with crisis
- from different personal life experiences

All of us in the industry were completely unaware of:

- what this fast-spreading, far-reaching, fatal virus was
- how to tame the beast
- how long the crisis would last
- how great the threat to the global community
- how grave the impact on lives and livelihoods

As we witnessed, responses varied dramatically, and to this day, many continue to react differently. There were leaders who chose to fight, those who stepped up, and also those who were unsure and/or unable to move forward then and still to this day.

CHAPTER 5

SMELLING SMOKE: RECOGNISING THE FIRST SIGNS OF TROUBLE

It was probably the end of January, early February. I was sitting in the British Airways boardroom for our IAG management committee meeting. We were talking about what was happening in Wuhan, China. This was before it had started spreading to Italy. We were looking at our plans and I said to the guys, 'This feels like this could be bad. This could be worse than maybe we had expected, I think we've got to start planning for some changes now.'

WILLIE WALSH, DIRECTOR GENERAL,
INTERNATIONAL AIR TRANSPORT ASSOCIATION (IATA)

Understanding how our brains work in a moment of crisis is one thing. Channelling that understanding into helpful action is another. As revealed in the section on the basic working of the brain, the actions we take are often initiated before we have even begun to understand what is happening to us. By studying the leaders profiled in this book, we will come to understand that the human response to threats is multifaceted. We react both consciously and subconsciously, making it a complex process. How we sense trouble, therefore, has a powerful role to play in how we respond. There may be nothing overly demanding of our attention, nothing that indicates we should be cautious. There may be no proof that something is wrong. There may be no visible detail, open discussion, or valid data. And yet we can sense something is going wrong, very wrong. We know we can smell smoke.

In the case of the pandemic, the signs of smoke were evident, even if they were coming from far away. For the first time in our lifetimes, large-scale warnings were emerging. A spread of illness, something beyond the seasonal norm, was happening. An illness that would be an even greater threat if not properly understood. In what seemed like no time at all, the smoke revealed deeply frightening flames: fatalities, frantic searching for facts, previously unseen levels of fear amongst global healthcare officials. The flames spread wider and faster, escalating the intensity of danger. The world was watching, panicking, and waiting for someone to explain what was happening and what action to take.

Officially, firewalls started to be put in place in the hope of stopping the spread of smoke and preventing the spark of more flames. These firewalls included localised lockdowns and international border and airspace closures. There were those who were making decisions based on protection – the need to regain control, reduce risk and extinguish the flames. UN entities, government leaders and global medical professionals were drip-feeding information, visibly unsure about what was happening.

Waves of government-led decisions were made as the global travel and tourism community watched on. The world was about to be engulfed in flames. For how long, we did not know. We were unsure how far-reaching the crisis would be and how severely we as an industry would be burnt by being brought to an absolute standstill. We could not imagine what was ahead. We prayed for safety.

There was so much that needed to be understood. If infection rates grew, and with them panic, what did this mean? Will further lockdowns be imposed? Will more borders be closed? Will airlines be grounded? Will businesses be closed? Will hotels, restaurants and other places of play be shuttered? Will staff be furloughed, or worse? Will special events be cancelled? Will concerts go quiet? Will theatres go dark? Will sport be benched? Will couples at the end of the aisle have to wait to say, 'I do'? And for how long? How bad would this really be? How long could the travel industry – one that is responsible for 10% of jobs worldwide – wait and see? Even today, we will never forget that time of uncertainty.

For the vast majority of people, the immediate response was flight or freeze – get to where you need to, stay home, stay safe. And yet as the first signs of smoke emerged, some leaders immediately focused outwards to the greater 'we', seeking understanding beyond the baseline of safety. Why? Because embedded in their wiring is the fact that when a calling is heard, it must be answered. Fight is an instinctive response for these leaders. Therefore, immediately understanding how to manage the spread of the fire was their first priority.

CHOOSING TO FIGHT: UNDERSTANDING THE MOMENT

The journey from awareness of a threat (smelling smoke) to interpretation of risk (seeing flames) and taking action as a leader (stepping forward and into the flames) is central to accessing learnings that can help others find calm, focus and a course of action when facing a crisis. Whilst it can be intellectualised and calmly dissected into cautious stages, thoughts and actions, we must appreciate what it truly is: a choice to *fight*.

The fight response is hugely courageous, even if one does not realise it at the time. Why? Because it implicitly accepts the risk of:

- loss of possible safety for oneself and/or others
- injury to oneself and/or others
- failure, severely disappointing oneself and/or others

For this reason, understanding the moment of awareness of danger is vital. And for the rest of our lives, it can remain crystal clear. Especially when we are facing a crisis as unprecedented and unpredictable as a global pandemic.

All of us know where we were when our 'COVID moment' occurred – when we knew something was very wrong. These leaders were no different. In their interviews, the leaders shared the exact moment they could sense this crisis was different. Each of them remembered exactly when and where their moment occurred. It happened at different times, in different places, through different information, in different scenarios, at different stages of the spread of the virus, in different parts of the world, and in different ways. Without exception their recall was immediate and their words raw, the residue of emotion from that moment was still visible.

For many, the 'something is happening' sensation stops there. The sense of an emerging crisis is followed by a period of wait and see to get more understanding, to figure out what to do, to wait for your heart to stop pounding and mind to stop swirling, to be told by someone what to do.

Just wait.

These leaders dealt with the crucial moment differently than most. Something in them, in their wiring, pushed them past the personal emotion of the moment and into a state of immediate processing beyond the 'me', 'here', and 'now'. Despite the absence of information or direction, parts of their minds were springing into action once more, it was truly remarkable to observe. They could not wait, as instinctively revealed by Cyril Ranque of Expedia:

> *I must be honest because you had no data to lean on, you had no history, you had no past behaviour to rely on. It was all on the go and day-by-day decisions, especially around the cancellation and refund policies which impact customers and partners. It's hard in the middle of the fire to make the right decision. I would summarise it by saying what I had to do, and*

I don't know if I did it well, but I had to do it, was to move from being
a peace general to a war general. And a war general has to solve really
fast, has to accept that speed trumps perfection, has to accept mistakes for
the greater good. Not everybody is going to be happy with the decisions
you make but you have to make them. And from a team management
perspective, always thinking positive, creating excitement about our future
experience, the future for our employees, and also about the industry's future
so that we keep our best people in our industry.

Somehow these leaders took their awareness and immediately moved it forward to implications. Their minds delved into the mental gymnastics of 'if this is happening':

- What does it mean?
- What does it mean for me?
- What does it mean for my family?
- What does it mean for my business, my colleagues, my partners, and my customers?

Listening to these leaders, it was clear that their minds immediately dissected the implications of the challenge they were facing in that moment, and how it was going to impact the people that they most cared about. Especially the young ones, as shared by Rani Raad of CNN:

I had to explain it to my kids. When the UK kicked in with the lockdown
and I had to sit down specifically with Sophia, my eight-year-old at
the time, to explain to her what was going on and to couch the whole
thing with words and a very careful attention to emotion, to language,
to suggestions. Fifty million things were going on in my mind on how I
needed to explain to my eight-year-old what we were going through without
scarring her for life.

Each person relived the emotions they felt during the first days of realising there was a global threat. Though over a thousand days had passed since the outbreak, when interviewed everyone vividly remembered their moment as if it were yesterday. The intensity of the moment – the rush of adrenaline, the surprise, shock, sadness, fear and urgency – etched the experience in their minds. The vividness of their recollection enabled them to recall the precise details of their thoughts, actions and responses to the crisis and those for whom they acted.

THE MOMENT

The leaders profiled in this book may be very different, but there is something they all share: an acute awareness of the exact moment they knew something was wrong. As already explained, all the leaders were exposed to a video narrative before their interviews that took them back to those early days of the crisis. Once the video ended, they were each asked the first question – a question that immediately took them back to what has become a defining moment in their lives:

> WE ALL KNOW EXACTLY WHERE WE WERE WHEN WE HAD OUR 'COVID MOMENT' – WHEN WE KNEW SOMETHING WAS DIFFERENT THIS TIME, SOMETHING WAS VERY WRONG. WHAT WAS YOUR COVID MOMENT?

Reflecting on the moment provoked an immediate, visceral response. Their emotions were visible, their slowness of breath audible, their expressions raw, their words unpolished. Their memories were completely relatable because wherever they were in the world, and wherever we were in the world, we all lived through it. We can all remember exactly where we were when we had our 'COVID moment'.

Please remember that these leaders are typically seen and heard in professional circumstances. Rarely do these settings provide a platform for personal perspectives, especially those that are highly emotional, as these would be uncomfortable for the leader, and cross a professional line for the general audience. By trusting the interview process and feeling deeply respected for their personal point of view, the leaders shared unscripted and unfiltered thoughts, some of which surprised even themselves. Their sharing was deeply personal, rather than presenting themselves as mere public personas. They are saluted for the gift of their transparency, honesty, authenticity and humanity.

> *They reinforced a fundamental aspect of this book's premise: that leaders are human.*

In their recollections below, their words reveal how vividly they still recall 'the moment', not just the time, place and situation, but also the strength of emotion and speed of thought processes that they experienced.

LEADER: JULIA SIMPSON, PRESIDENT AND CEO, WTTC
HOME BASE: LONDON, UK

At the time I was working in aviation with International Airlines Group, and I'd been given permission by the government to continue going to work because we were deemed a critical service. Planes were still flying because they were flying some critical people and supplies around the world. It was critical to keep that network open. I remember walking from my home in central London to Paddington Station, I didn't see one soul. Not one car moving, not one human being. I got into Paddington Station and it was completely empty. In fact, I wondered if my train was even going to go, if there was a driver, I didn't see a soul. I think it was at that moment, I realised the power that the mix of the pandemic and the politics around the pandemic could create.

LEADER: FRED DIXON, CEO, NEW YORK CITY TOURISM + CONVENTIONS
HOME BASE: NEW YORK CITY, USA

We were monitoring it from really late December, as soon as it started to move in China, because it had an immediate impact on inbound Chinese business. We noticed it right away and activated our crisis team in early January. And then the city began to shut down, which we had not seen in that way before. The day that Broadway closed, we knew we were in for something. So many people were looking to us for answers that we didn't have. The only thing we could do was to prepare our colleagues in the industry for the worst possible scenario. Many people were calling me day and night and saying, 'This is going to be like two weeks, right?' I mean, I just closed my shop. I just shut down my operation, sent people home. And I said, 'I don't think so. I think that we need to prepare for a much longer run.'

LEADER: GAVIN TOLLMAN, CEO, THE TRAVEL CORPORATION
HOME BASE: GENEVA, SWITZERLAND

I was having dinner with some friends and the young lady who was serving us came up and she was crying, and she said they have just shut the borders to Italy. She was Italian and was so worried about her parents. She said she didn't know what was going on and she couldn't go back. It was in that instant I realised the enormity of the impact on humanity. Because what I saw in this young lady was absolute total terror. She did not know what to do. She did not know how to respond.

I still recall how I felt this sinking feeling all the way into the pit of my stomach because I understood instantaneously what this meant for our business.

LEADER: MARLOES KNIPPENBERG, CEO, KERTEN HOSPITALITY
HOME BASE: MILAN, ITALY

I still remember leaving Saudi Arabia. I left twenty-four hours before they closed the country for over a year, thinking that I could potentially stay two, three weeks. Everything would be fine after and go from there. Arriving in Istanbul, it started to be daunting as we were, again, having more guests who were leaving as the lockdown started. As it continued, I had to make a decision to stay with my team in the business or go home and see what would happen. I decided to stay with my team in the business in Istanbul for almost six weeks. It was one of those moments where I thought, 'if I am not here, if I can't touch, if I cannot be with the people in the middle of it, I'm not sure we'll have a business after'. I did not understand or could foresee the dimensions and how long it was really going on. I think if I would not have taken that decision, I think if fear would've hit me or if my first priority was going home, I'm not sure we would have a business today at the dimension that we have it today. And if you would ask me, would I do it again exactly the same way? Yes, a hundred per cent.

LEADER: HON. PREMIER WINDE,
PREMIER OF THE WESTERN CAPE, SOUTH AFRICA
HOME BASE: CAPE TOWN, SOUTH AFRICA

I think my moment was probably about forty-eight hours before South Africa went into lockdown. I had already pulled our team together. It was on a Sunday, and I said, if you see what's happening in Wuhan and now you see what's happening in Italy, what are we going to do about it? And basically, we worked out our plan. We'd worked on our plan and moved on two weeks, and I was actually holding a disaster management meeting. I had the full cabinet there. I had all our heads of department. I had all our disaster people and we had a couple of epidemiologists and professors from our universities. We were having our discussion of what our readiness was. I got a message to say that the president will be calling you to have a discussion because in the next forty-eight hours we're probably going to have to go into a lockdown.

LEADER: PROFESSOR DEMIAN HODARI, EHL HOSPITALITY BUSINESS SCHOOL, LAUSANNE
HOME BASE: LAUSANNE, SWITZERLAND

I think it's when I was talking to my kids about it. It must have been like early February because I had just come back from the States on a flight. I said I think this is going to be bad, especially because we can transmit it without even knowing we have it. They said their biology teacher told them the opposite; it's just a cold, it's a light flu, they're blowing it out of proportion. I thought that's not at all what I'm reading. I got concerned that there were different perspectives or interpretations of the science and there was so much uncertainty. That's when I got more worried, when I realised not everyone is seeing this the same way.

LEADER: MATTHEW UPCHURCH, CEO, VIRTUOSO
HOME BASE: TEXAS, USA

We were about to celebrate the twentieth anniversary of the Virtuoso brand, which was born in 2000. Our team of three of our executives had come back from Shanghai for a visit in January. Our team there had said that they were wearing masks because something was going on but that they were not sure what was happening. Then we had our US-Canada forum in late January, early February, the stock market dropped 600 points that Friday when it ended because of the beginnings of this. I actually said 'pandemic' in that speech. And what I remember so incredibly well is that we had never in the history of our organisation cancelled a major event.

LEADER: MALCOLM HENDRY, RED CARNATION HOTELS COLLECTION
HOME BASE: LONDON, UK

It was July the fourth. We had a few months of it. I'd seen London streets decimated, that actually was bad enough. It's when we opened our doors for the first time. I'd been in London long enough, twenty-plus years. I've been through recessions and financial crises. I've been through unique events like the London bombings, 9/11 and all life up until then had thrown at us. London always bounces back. Resilience, strength. We think, July the fourth we open the doors, and the bookings will pile in. We'll go back to normal. We opened the doors, and nothing happened. Nothing happened. Then you knew that something was different. That three-week period that we tried to get things going because, if you think about logistically and just practically, there weren't any flights coming across, so where's all this business coming from? But we were so London institutionalised, they're going to come to London. They just didn't come, you knew that something was very, very different. Those three weeks that we were open were probably the hardest three weeks that I've had.

LEADER: WILLIE WALSH, DIRECTOR GENERAL, IATA
HOME BASE: LONDON, UK (AT THE TIME)

It was actually quite early in the whole pandemic. It was probably the end of January, early February. I was sitting in the British Airways boardroom for our IAG management committee meeting. We were talking about what was happening in Wuhan, China. This was before it had started spreading to Italy. We were looking at our plans and I said to the guys, 'This feels like this could be bad. This could be worse than maybe we had expected, I think we've got to start planning for some changes now.' I suppose this comes from having lived through a few crises in the airline industry and particularly having seen how the industry reacted badly to some downturns. It had started with us having to cancel flights into China, which wasn't a big part of our network, but it was just to me, a bell going off in my head.

Their COVID moments throw open a window into how the minds of these leaders worked as fighters. To read their words is to hear their voices, see their worlds, feel their heartbeats, sense how the wheels in their minds were starting to spin, realising they needed to fight and how their fight needed to be about protecting more than just themselves. Their innate filters were activated, pushing past fear to find a place of focus. In their own ways, they show how their lenses zoomed in on what they deemed to be critical steps to, first and foremost, establish safety within their world, both personally and professionally.

> *The line between professional and personal was immediately erased. This is a hallmark of any major crisis – the personal self and the professional self become one.*

These people are no longer business cards.

They are no longer leaders.

They are human beings that have chosen to step up and fight.

They have found within themselves the clarity and confidence to face the flames.

Their mission is to establish safety for the greater 'we', doing everything in their power to make sure as many as possible get through unburned.

CHAPTER 6

LOCATING THE EMERGENCY EXIT: DEFINING PRIORITIES

The most pressing need was what did we need to do for our guests? How do we get people home? I haven't thought about this in a while. People were just getting stranded. Airlines were stopping taking people. We had thousands of people all over the world. 'How are we going to repatriate people who are everywhere?' was one of our core considerations.

GAVIN TOLLMAN, CEO, THE TRAVEL CORPORATION (TTC)

Central to taking control of the moment was the focus on safety. This was not only about physical safety and protection against the risk of the virus. As the world started to shut down, panic arose around the need to get to the place where it was safe to be stuck. This was critical, especially considering that many of us lived in a world of constant travel.

The focus for most of the leaders interviewed became about ensuring that their leaders, and those they were leading, were safely in places where they knew they were not only at minimal personal risk, but also where they knew they had some control over the increasingly unnerving situation. Dan Richards of Global Rescue said:

We started taking measures to prepare our company and our employees and the families of our employees for what we thought was to come. None of us could have predicted exactly the trajectory of this, the level of transmission, the lethality, how this would play out over the next couple of years. We prepared for the worst, and for us in our business, we're in the crisis business.

Our mandate, our pledge is to be there for our clients and members when they need it most, and we can't do that unless we're able to take care of ourselves first. So, we did all the things that I thought we needed to do, even though we were well postured going into this, but adding to the specific threats that we were going to be dealing with, regarding PPE, enhanced communications capabilities, augmenting our satellite, telephone and data capabilities, making sure that our operation centres had sufficient food, fuel, water access, weapons, ammunition. Everything that you could imagine that might be needed for a very serious and protracted engagement with this virus and the potential breakdown of social order in these places.

Very soon, it was clear that the world was facing a crisis much longer lasting than anyone expected or was prepared for, and businesses needed to prepare to take cover for the long haul. Leaders knew it was their responsibility to create some sense of stability, even with all the unknowns that continued to emerge. Were the people they were responsible for feeling secure? Were they feeling productive? Were they able to focus forward, looking at signs of confidence and positivity rather than getting completely enveloped by fear and paranoia?

The mental health component of the pandemic rapidly became a global concern as not only were people struggling with the lockdown physically, but they were also struggling psychologically. Why? Because while lockdowns sought to limit the movement of people as a way of controlling the spread of the virus, the extended periods that people had to endure in restricted, unchanging spaces inflicted a severe limitation on thought and freedom. In many cases, this caused enormous anxiety for people who needed external stimulus, fresh air, exercise, social interaction – and to know that they were still in control. In those days, control meant maintaining a productive, purposeful, hopeful routine. This was especially true for those in the hospitality industry.

Malcolm Hendry of Red Carnation Hotels emphasised the importance of confidence and momentum in the hospitality industry. He stressed that visible leadership on the front line is vital to building and maintaining that confidence and momentum:

> *I've always thought that when you are called out, when situations call you, the best thing, the right thing, the real leader type of thing is to put yourself there in front of everyone and be able to answer the questions and say to people, 'Yes, we're closed, but I am here.' All the agents that we called, I didn't call them from home. I called them from the hotel. I made a point of calling them from the hotel. I made a point of switching the lights on, filling the champagne buckets, putting things out. It wasn't a closed hotel. That was an important message. I chose to do it. And I wanted them to see me here. Not that they could book us in any way, but to be reassured that The Rubens at the Palace Hotel are still here, Hotel 41 is still here, Bbar is still here, and we are ready to go when people allow us to go.*

First and foremost, as evidenced by their immediate responses, leaders processed exactly what establishing safety meant.

TAKING THE SAFETY OF THEIR PEOPLE PERSONALLY

But why did they do it? Why was it the responsibility of these leaders to take responsibility for the safety of others? What was behind their motivation to fight? This is an important aspect of the lessons that these leaders provide.

A calling to leadership in a crisis mobilises a leader into action in a way that goes beyond their job description. The call of duty to lead in a time of crisis is based on an innate sense of responsibility towards the trust others place in them. In the case of the leaders interviewed, this included responsibility extended to:

- their peers: staff, customers, partners, stakeholders
- their bosses: royal families, government leaders, boards of directors
- their friends and family

Each of them knew that this was a call of duty they had to answer. Why? Because it is who they are, it was how they are wired.

Success was not about professional success. It was not about making sure that certain KPIs were met. Success came down to the fundamental definition of safety: calming fear, helping people through the storm, and importantly, helping others see beyond the storm. Ultimately, they knew that once the storm had passed, which they knew it would, they needed to be able to look their people in the eye and know they had done all they could when their calling came. Equally important, they needed to be able to look at themselves in the mirror and acknowledge that they answered the call.

As Paul Griffiths of DAA explained:

> *When you are in that position where you're given no alternative but to lead somehow, I think you find that resource from within to lead. I wouldn't say I was afraid, but I think I was uncertain at times. I think I very, very rarely let that uncertainty surface because I knew to be a leader and to inspire confidence and reassurance in the thousands of staff that depended on me, being a leader was a more powerful, motivating force than the fear within me.*

Darrell Wade of Intrepid said:

> *I think that's just a natural reaction and maybe it's the CEO mentality.*
> *CEOs are very good at looking at a situation, assessing a problem, and*
> *wanting to solve it. Whether they can or not is a different story, but they*
> *instantly go to solutions and wanting to solve things.*

Willie Walsh of IATA explained:

> *I'd announced my retirement in January. So, I was planning to retire at the*
> *end of March, then this all kicked off. So, despite the fact I was planning*
> *to retire, I said, 'No, we've got to take leadership here.'*

Fahd Hamidaddin of STA:

> *From the crisis, I was able to see leaders distinguished by two qualities,*
> *one is their ability to change their habits and embark into the unknown.*
> *And the second is when no one takes responsibility and [they] lead by*
> *acting, by taking charge.*

Malcolm Hendry of Red Carnation Hotels said:

> *I didn't work from home. I wanted to come into the hotel. I'm not passing*
> *it. My role doesn't make sense at home. I could have worked from home. I*
> *could have had quite an easy time at home actually. I could have an easier*
> *time, but it's not what I thought was right.*

In many cases, the immediate response was to build security and confidence internally. 'Protecting our people', which included partners and other external entities closely aligned to the organisation's community, was the call to action. Being safe, however, does not have a stop point. As a crisis evolves, so too do the elements needing to be taken safely through.

But how does a leader decide what is most important to focus on? And when? It's all about prioritisation. Interestingly, what to prioritise emerges as vividly and rapidly as what *not* to prioritise.

PRIORITISATION

When trouble was detected and the leaders were faced with a threat, they had the ability to immediately prioritise establishing a position of safety first and foremost. Once there was peace of mind that immediate safety concerns had been addressed, they were very quick to shift their focus and get down to business.

What were the priorities? For some, crises experienced in the past rapidly revealed priorities in the present, and learnings were applied. For others without the benefit of hindsight and war wounds from battles previously fought, there was a need to immediately make sense of the growing madness, to make the right decisions in the moment, for that moment in time. This decision differed according to the part of the industry. What did not differ was leaders' clarity.

In aviation the priority was one thing and one thing only, according to Willie Walsh of IATA:

> *Liquidity in our industry is absolutely critical. You get into that classic case of a spiral where people are cancelling flights and people are not booking. The outflow of cash starts really fast. I'd seen it before. Having seen what had happened in 2001 post 9/11, having witnessed 2008, 2009, which were the two sort of major crises. On scale crises that we had seen previously, liquidity was absolutely key and taking measures to secure liquidity had to be the number one decision. Then it was all the associated decisions.*

In travel sales the priority was different, as Cyril Ranque of Expedia described:

> *It hit us very, very quickly because we went from a nice gross trajectory to a cliff where we were receiving millions and millions of cancellation calls. Literally, you're going from money coming in the door to money going out the door overnight in proportions that are ridiculous, like hundreds of millions of dollars going out the door. So, we had to be quick.*
>
> *Priority #1 was how to save the company because if you don't achieve priority number one, then nothing else matters.*
>
> *Priority #2 was how to save relationships with customers and partners.*
>
> *Priority #3 was accepting OK, it's a crisis, but we can never waste a good crisis. So, what do we do to stay ahead of the curve? I think the number one priority saved the company.*

THE INNER CIRCLE

As the leaders have demonstrated, with clear priorities it becomes about identifying one's 'inner circle' – who they want near them to ensure safety and to achieve a successful outcome. Why was this so important? Simply this:

> *Good leaders have the wisdom and humility to know that they cannot take on a crisis on their own.*

All leaders need people they can turn to for honest, actionable intel, insight, and, particularly, inspiration. Why inspiration? Knowing the natural pressure, fear and fatigue that leading in a crisis brings on, inspiration can in fact become the most valuable element. So, a leader quietly asks themselves:

- Who are the people that can be trusted?
- Who are the people that are respected for their intelligence, their spirit, their focus and their fight?
- Who are the people that will be brutally honest?
- Who will be of support with no agenda?
- Who will deflect drama?
- Who are the people they truly know and who know them?

In a crisis, there is no time and energy for people to focus on anything but what is required – to stop the bleeding or the spread of fear and anxiety, and in turn, stop operational, financial and other damage. This may sound obvious, but let's pause for a moment and think about what we are really talking about here.

Leadership is incredibly demanding, especially when a crisis occurs. Leaders are expected to be the source of confidence, comfort, information, direction, strength, compassion and well-being for others. Leaders are expected to know everything, to have a plan and to see through the fire even when everyone else's eyes are thick with smoke. But the truth is that the position of leadership is a very lonely one. It can be a very scary one. It is a highly, highly pressurised one. And it is a thankless one.

Therefore, especially when a crisis hits, leaders must never feel alone. They too need someone to go to for strength, confidence, comfort, insight, compassion and well-being. They need someone to protect them while they are busy protecting others. Protection may simply be having someone to turn to and say, 'I'm scared' or admit, 'I don't know', or even reveal, 'I have COVID'. It may be a person to turn to for a hug of strength, a safe space to quietly rebuild their reserves. These people become, in many ways, the renewable battery pack that every leader needs to have within them.

One of the most touching stories of a remarkable pandemic-time leader revealing the importance of their inner circle came long before I started writing this book. It was December 2020, during the thick of the first COVID-19 wave. A private conversation was being had with Hon. Premier Alan Winde, premier of the Western Cape, South Africa (profiled in this book) and his beautiful First Lady, Tracy. The question was asked to both: what did you learn about each other that you had never recognised before?

Tracy responded very honestly, saying that she didn't realise how broad her husband's shoulders were. She then added that she also had not realised how much the pressure on his shoulders impacted her.

The Hon. Premier spoke without hesitation: he never realised how much he needed the First Lady.

Interestingly, one of the insights from the creation of this book was that as much as the twenty leaders interviewed had done hundreds of interviews over the pandemic, no one had ever gone beyond asking questions about their industry, their economy, or their people, to simply ask 'How are you?' The interviews for *The Call to Leadership* seemed, in many ways, the first time that leaders were asked at a very personal and human level: how are you?

Those chosen to be in the 'inner circle' may not be in leadership positions in the organogram. Whether to support leaders in government or business, those chosen offered the perfect combination of substance, style, spirit, sensibility and sensitivity. Gavin Tollman of TTC said:

> *We convened an urgent meeting in London. The family flew in, and we*
> *met at The Milestone where we made some conscious decisions. I don't*
> *think any of us realised at all at that moment how long this was going to*

last. One of the first key decisions we turned to was that of our team, our people: we understood in that instant we needed to look after our teams. So, consciously we went out of our way to start giving our team members, our people, an understanding that we would be looking to support them through this period. Having individuals by my side, having individuals within our team, that I knew that I could talk to, who could get things done was an imperative.

Alan Winde, premier of the Western Cape, described his inner circle:

I actually put a team together. I got one of my ministers who was the most military out of everybody, but I didn't keep him there for very long. I removed him from it because he was too militaristic, and this was about people. That was when I said, OK, I'm changing this. I'm going to step in. This is how it's going to work. Sundays are for strategy. Mondays, Wednesdays and Fridays are cabinet meetings, but extended cabinet are incorporated into our cabinet meetings, every region of the province. All mayors and municipal managers, but we also brought in the military. We brought in the police. We brought in national departments who don't normally sit in our cabinets either. We put them all into the space that said every single week, we are going to get a report back for you. You can talk to your people who you can get the message across, the whole of our province, everywhere it's needed. This will be the management structure.

Kimarli Fernando of Sri Lanka's tourism board described being part of an inner circle:

When there was COVID-19 in China and other countries, the president appointed a group of people to be in the COVID-19 task force. It was a few people in health, a few people in the military, myself, the police, immigration, some from the export development board, and the president himself leading it. Then we realised one of our tour guides for our Italian guests who came to Sri Lanka had got it. That day we went into lockdown, I was saying, 'But I will open for tourists.' And everyone said, 'What, are you crazy?' I said, 'No, I will open for tourists in a safe way.' At the highest level there was a commitment. I spoke to every single one of them in the Ministry of Health to build rapport with them and because I didn't know them before. They bought into the idea that tourism is important. Three million people are dependent on us. We convinced them by showing them that we will open it with a secure bio bubble, that nobody will have any contact with citizens of Sri Lanka except the hotels.

We convinced them. Every single hotel was visited. Every single hotel was audited. Every single staff member in the hotel was trained. Every single driver, every single guide, every single travel agent was trained. I looked at other countries like Singapore. I looked at Dubai, I looked at Japan. I just read, read, read, read, read, and then changed things.

In all cases, leaders knew immediately what the cost of grounding the global travel and tourism industry was. They knew the commercial implications of borders and skies closing, and business grinding to an immediate halt. They knew the risk that would come to the employees. And they knew the risk to the lives and livelihoods of their people.

They also knew what they needed to do,

why,

when,

and with whom.

Then it was about rising to the moment and taking action.

CHAPTER 7

WIRED TO LEAD: HONOURING THE LEADER WITHIN

To me it is a very personal thing.
And it was something that I wanted to defend.
I wanted everyone here in authority to feel that at all times the
airport and the team that worked for me, and all of the things
we were responsible for doing here, was 100% dependable in
a world that was very, very strange and unreadable.

PAUL GRIFFITHS, CEO, DUBAI AIRPORTS AUTHORITY (DAA)

As we know from our own experiences, when a threat is detected, the human response is primal. In the moment it can be impossible to think beyond the immediate. We find it impossible to separate ourselves from fear, anxiety and the noise. Our thought processes are dramatically simplified and accelerated. The focus is on our own survival. The emphasis is on our physical state of well-being. It's natural because in the moment it is scary. Critically, our personal wiring becomes super-charged, sparking us to immediately ask:

- What exactly is the threat? What is going on?
- How at risk am I, really? Is it direct or indirect, a justified feeling of danger or instinctive panic?
- Where is safety? Do I need to remove myself from somewhere? Someone?
- Who is safety? Is there someone, somewhere, I need to go to for help?
- Once I feel 'safe', then what do I do?

This primal response is natural. The last thing we should ever do is blame ourselves for it, especially when, as outlined in the section about how the human brain responds to crisis, sensing danger automatically unlocks this primal response. The physical 'me' matters first. This is why it is completely understandable that only once a person feels a sense of calm and control, then they can widen their focus to others – the greater 'we'.

Who makes up the 'we'? This is an interesting aspect of crisis response. It can surprise us who we think of when we look to protect others. It may be family, friends, colleagues, staff or students. Whoever it is, it is those we feel are counting on us to care for them. Immediately, instinctively, we seek to establish:

- Where are they?
- What risk are they facing?
- What do I need to do to get them to safety?
- Is there anyone else counting on me to protect them?
- Who can I count on?
- What do I need to do? What are my priorities?

The lens widens more and more until it reaches a point where people realise they have done enough and can say, 'I have helped enough'. This feeling is natural and understandable. Typically, the stopping point is immediate family – those for whom an emotional responsibility is felt.

As we saw in early 2022, not only did the virus prove to be highly infectious, but it also created a wave of fear terrifying enough to stop the world. Within the global travel and tourism leadership community, we saw many leaders step back. Many needed to focus on their immediate sphere of influence. Many struggled to find the ability to focus. It was an incredibly difficult time. We didn't know what we were facing. We didn't know how long it would last, and we certainly did not know the degree of damage the crisis would inflict.

And we certainly did not know what others were facing. We had no way of knowing what was happening in the lives of those people we were exposed to, primarily online. We did not know the pressure they were under, the pain they were facing, the tightness of proximity or the isolation of distance they were feeling, the concerns they had for their jobs, and the concern they had for their own loved ones. As shared by Dr Gupta,

> *The thing about something like a pandemic is that the suffering that happens at the time when lives are lost, when people get very sick, so much of that suffering happens behind closed doors, behind closed doors to your house, doors to hospitals, doors to morgues, doors to religious organisations. So there's no centre of grief.*

Many were facing immediate challenges that needed their direct attention. They could only focus on the 'me' because the threats to the 'me' were so severe. They were not able to answer the call to leadership of the 'we'. And that's OK – their wiring yielded reactions of flight and freeze. No one should ever be judged for their wiring or their situation. We will look more closely at this innate response later in the book. Here and now we focus on those whose wiring unlocked within them the choice to fight – those who needed to help others.

Being unable to stop working did not, however, come without a pause. At some point early on in their response a pause would have had to take place, a pause that would make time and space for one of the toughest conversations they would ever have during the crisis, a pause needed to confirm that stepping forward, even in the face of risk, was their firm decision: a conversation with themselves.

THE TOUGH CONVERSATION

By default, we think about leaders in times of crisis from the outside in. We don't look at them from the inside out. We don't consider what it means for a leader to make the choice to step up and lead. We know that there is an instinctive response to a calling, a sense of needing to do something, to step forward, to help others. What is easy to forget, however, is the hard conversation that leaders must have with themselves when deciding to lead in a crisis, especially when there is direct risk to themselves.

Why is this conversation so hard? Because it is very easy for loved ones, colleagues, partners and people around the leader to ask, 'Why you?'

Their question is valid. Why do you need to step up? Why do you need to be the one losing sleep? Why do you need to be the saviour? Why does it have to be you?

> *At some point, a leader needs to be able to say to themself and those around them, 'I must do this. It must be me, and this is why.'*

To be able to dive into the thought process of a leader when they choose to step up is an important aspect of understanding their experience. Leadership during a crisis can be incredibly scary, risky and vulnerable. What's more, it can be incredibly isolating. When leaders step up in crisis, they know that they are most likely stepping forward on their own. They may have people around them that support them and who are counting on them, people they do not wish to disappoint. They feel their support, but still these leaders know that they alone must take on the hard decisions, have the hard conversations, and take the hard first steps towards the eye of the storm.

This requires that leaders carefully assess the degree of risk to themselves.

What is the physical risk?

Are they going to be hurt?

What is the long-term impact on themselves, and on others?

There's also the emotional risk. If they do this, what is going to happen to them?

What does this mean for them?

How are they going to remember this time?

And critically, if they don't do anything, how will they remember this time?

Will they accept their action or inaction?

It was clear during the interviews that leaders had these tough conversations with themselves, even if subconsciously. They knew their leadership would be a solitary experience. Despite their inner circle of trusted friends and colleagues, they knew that they would have to make hard decisions on their own. They knew that they were being observed. They knew that there were those around them, looking to them for strength and confidence. And there was the possibility others were looking at them with envy and a competitive ego. These leaders knew they needed to step up and saw it as their duty, a calling to which they had to respond and honour:

- the title of leadership they possessed
- those who had entrusted them to lead
- what was not only required of them but expected of them
- their calling

As articulated by Cyril Ranque of Expedia, in a crisis our wiring to work becomes a key resource for establishing the focus needed right now, letting go of the busyness, prioritising the essential business:

> *I think to some extent it's a personality thing. It's simpler. I have a personality that is more at ease in a high-pressure environment than in a low-pressure environment, so it makes your decision simpler, quicker.*

I remember when I told you this quote about moving from a 'peace general' to a 'war general'. In a corporate environment, when you are in peace times, you have a lot of peripheral things to do. You have your business targets, your employees, etc., but the system creates a lot of additional tasks and additional sub-focused areas. When it's a crisis, all this goes away and it's about, what is the most important, next thing that I can do. And let's not have twenty different important next things that you can do for your team or for different parts of your team. Let's put everybody on the same target so that you can execute it extremely fast, extremely well.

Importantly, these leaders could see beyond the pandemic. They were able to see the world not only after the crisis but *stronger* because of the crisis. And not just stronger as businesses but stronger as people. This is where so many of the leaders interviewed stood out, because they showed compassion to ensure that others also came through stronger. It was their wiring, who they were as leaders, as demonstrated by Rani Raad of CNN:

For me, rallying around the troops when COVID kicked in just felt like a natural thing. That was my first reaction – to reach out to those people to say, 'Look, I know you're dealing with this, and now you've got that on top of it. What can I do?'

As Rani infers, this wiring was initially set and reinforced thereafter through the chapters of their lives.

LEADERS AND THEIR DEFINING MOMENTS

At the heart of this book is the following thesis, a human truth that I fundamentally believe: those hearing a call to lead have, at some time in their lives, had an experience that not only revealed their willingness to face a crisis with clarity and courage, but firmly set their wiring. These moments become a bookmark in one's life story, stored in the brain's memory bank. The importance of these moments is not solely the detail of the 'what', 'where', 'when' and 'who'. It is the 'how' that is critical – how the moment was comprehended, confronted and overcome. The 'how' is what becomes embedded in our wiring. It's importance is so strong that it defines instinctive response. In the 'how', who we are is anchored.

These defining moments will always be there, strongly influencing our values, principles and priorities, and as a result, our instinctive responses.

These moments come to define what matters to us in the world and how we engage with the world.

These defining experiences can be positive or negative, moments of great joy or great sadness. They have such an impact that they can fundamentally shape our identity and can occur at any time in our life. Why do I so firmly believe this? Because I have lived it. I have my moment. 23 September 1994, 6.40 p.m. Central Africa time. Then, there, my wiring was set. And it is a wiring that has defined my response to crisis, and life in general, ever since.

To apply this firm belief and test this book's thesis, the leaders were all asked a stirring question. It was asked following the discussion around when their 'COVID moment' occurred and their immediate, intuitive response to sensing they were facing a crisis. It was asked knowing they were being asked to dig deep.

> YOUR RESPONSE WHEN COVID HIT DIRECTLY REFLECTS YOUR WIRING, HOW YOU INSTINCTIVELY STEP FORWARD TO LEAD WHEN YOU ARE FACED WITH A CRISIS. WAS THERE A MOMENT IN YOUR PAST, SOMETHING THAT HAPPENED, THAT YOU BELIEVE SET YOUR WIRING?

The leaders allowed me into different chapters of their lives, taking us back to defining moments to help understand their wiring. For some, their stories came from the early days when they were young children. For others, it was later during their school years, whether primary, secondary, tertiary, or even thereafter. And for others, it was during their professional career.

The leaders have an exceptional ability to read people, quickly identifying the attitudes, ambitions and agendas of others. They carefully control what they share about themselves with others, both professionally and personally. In public, very few of the defining chapters of their lives are revealed. And why is this? Not only because of their desire to keep their private lives private, but also because those in the professional world know there is a line they cannot cross. It would be inappropriate and unprofessional. And so, they stay out.

Remarkably, every one of the leaders profiled in this book allowed me unique, deeply personal access to chapters in their lives that they feel have shaped them not only as professionals but as people. Their reactions to a challenging experience, or several experiences, set their wiring and their wiring mobilised these leaders into action when their 'COVID moment' occurred. Significantly, their life chapters help us reconsider the defining moments in our own lives, strengthening our understanding of:

- what these moments demanded of us in terms of thoughts and actions
- how we or they responded
- the wiring that has occurred within us as a result

It was exciting for some of the leaders to reflect on their chapters and hear themselves share their moments out loud – the where, when, why and with whom. They had never before framed those chapters that way for themselves. For other leaders, however, it was deeply disturbing. For all, it was clearly moving.

WIRED BY TRAINING

For some leaders, their responses make it clear that their wiring was set when they were focused on building their careers. Their early professional training embedded wiring that enabled them to navigate through a storm. Willie Walsh of IATA said:

> *My training as a pilot helped because when you're in the air and you have to make a decision, you don't have the luxury of saying, well, just hang around up here for a while because you'll run out of fuel. So, you have a limited amount of time in which to decide what you're going to do.*

Likewise, the ongoing training one receives from failing may be significant, Dan Richards of Global Rescue, reminds us:

> *Honestly, failure and repeated failure, and then overcoming failure, is the key. And I hate to say it, but you know, I don't think that we do as good a job today as we have done in decades past at embracing failure. Failing, and then coming back from those failures, creates resilience and that breeds resilient people. I've been a lifelong athlete and I can tell you that athletes are better at this than I think almost anyone.*

WIRED TO SERVE

Some leaders have a strong sense of responsibility that stems from serving a select group of individuals they deeply respect, feel obliged to, and appreciate. They are dedicated to the service of a greater vision, mission, identity and set of values. It is a sense of responsibility that brings them great clarity, strength and pride, especially in times of challenge when they know others are looking to them with trust, confidence and gratitude.

All the leaders interviewed shed light on how powerful this sense of service can be. Their response to the crisis is what inspired the title of this book – it is a calling. In some cases, it is a call of duty to the service of royalty, as revealed by Paul Griffiths of DAA:

I think there's nothing more energising than having the trust and responsibility given to you, in my case by a member of the royal family of the ruling party here. I'm always driven by the fact that the worst feeling in the world is when you let someone down. If someone on whom you depend has let you down, you're put in the most unenviable position imaginable because, through no fault of your own, you have let someone down and you've relied on someone who has betrayed your trust. I saw that if I failed in any way to deliver on that promise of making largely the right decisions, and I'm not going to say for a moment they were all the right decisions, but if I had failed the UAE government, by making the wrong decisions, I will have betrayed their trust in me as a human being. And that to me is a very personal thing. And it was something that I wanted to defend.

I wanted everyone here in authority to feel that at all times that the airport and the team that worked for me, and all of the things we were responsible for doing here, was 100% dependable in a world that was very, very strange and unreadable. And I felt that that gave me the strength because here you see, I'm not just an employee. I am here to fulfil a very significant social responsibility, and that is to provide leadership and development and guidance to the people who work for me.

Many people outside look at Dubai Airport as an example, as a great employer, as a professional organisation, as a ground-breaking leader in so many fields. And I felt that social responsibility during the pandemic was the thing that motivated me most of all, but also gave me strength because I was always judging this based on, we've got a macro situation that's incredibly difficult to read, but I was never unsure at all about what my responsibilities were towards the people who work for me and towards the government who were desperate to get travel and tourism back on track here.

Similarly, there are those serving long-established family businesses that are, in their country and even around the world, regarded as royalty, as is the case with India's Tata family, ably served by Puneet Chhatwal of IHCL:

This very much ties in with the values of the Tata group. I don't think that I would've necessarily responded that way or in that magnitude if I was not part of this group. I mean, here, it's from the founder's philosophy that everything revolves around the community that you come from. And it's about giving back to where you came from.

For these leaders, the pain of disappointing their leaders – their elders – is a pain too harsh to contemplate.

WIRED BY TRAGEDY

Then there are those whose call to serve was wired as a result of a past traumatic situation – a crisis they had survived – that has had a deep, personal impact on who they are today. Having made it through, these leaders knew that they could make it through anything they faced because they had gone through worse in the past. As aptly stated by Fahd Hamidaddin, of STA, even in the darkest of times, the opportunity to learn provides light:

I'm a strong believer that when everything is easy and everything is successful, celebrate success, but when everything is tough and challenging, appreciate the learning. Remember to focus on, and to capture, the learning. That will only make you a better version of yourself after that challenge passes.

All the leaders interviewed across the world were generous in sharing how their thinking has been shaped, their wiring set. Their shared thoughts were highly intimate, their responses even taking them by surprise as they made the connection, in some instances for the first time. For two of our leaders, their wiring was set when their nations were attacked – a situation that directly threatened the future safety and well-being of themselves, and their loved ones. For Kimarli Fernando, of Sri Lanka's tourism board, it was the experience of growing up in war-torn Sri Lanka and surviving as a proud, purposeful national that embedded her wiring:

> *For me personally, I feel that it is my value system. My belief, we are courageous. I think many of us are courageous. We've experienced a lot in our life through the war. We lost friends. We lost people, myself, my family. My father was kidnapped, and I had to negotiate his release. Everybody said, you cannot have him alive. I said I will. His life depended on me. When the police told me, 'You'll never be able to. You have to pay the ransom but then they will kill him.' I said, 'No.' This was duty. Right? It was nothing to do with the war, but it was, they were just kidnapping people who had some wealth or whatever. These experiences where someone's life depends on you, you feel at that time, duty. During COVID I felt three million people relied on me.*

In Kenya, the Hon. Najib Balala's moment came when confronting and overcoming a crisis that shaped national unity and stability:

> *You don't expect these things to happen until when you're in it and they happen. Not because you have planned it, but because it's your instinct. You know that COVID was the invisible enemy. In the Westgate Mall shooting [of 2013] we knew who the enemy was: ISIS and Al Shabab. With COVID, I sit with you, and we are safe, tomorrow we are sick. So, these are the things that made us think differently to Al Shabab.*

For Rani Raad of CNN, growing up in war-ravaged Lebanon, childhood simply was what it was:

> *I grew up in war for the first seven years of my life. The war had started in 1975. I was born in 1976 in Dubai. We stayed there for a few months to about a year, and then we were back in Lebanon in 1977. So, in 1977, all the way through to 1984, I think it was, I grew up in a world where we would be in class and then we would be rushed to shelters, and we didn't have sirens and things like that. This was Lebanon. This isn't a sophisticated sort of country. The shelling starts, get the kids, and go to the shelter. So, I spent a lot of time in shelters. I spent a lot of time in different places, like in basements of buildings and bathtubs of bathrooms whenever the shelling started. That's just the way it was.*

It was by virtue being Lebanese and living in Lebanon at the time. For me it's this fight or flight kind of thing where we always, well, we couldn't run, and we couldn't fight. So, we just did something.

Some of us went through something that caused us to become a little bit more resilient, but also compassionate; compassionate, but also brave; brave but also fearful for the people around us because you care for their well-being. It just created so many different emotions for us as kids and sort of forty years later, as I reflect on that, and this is probably the first time I speak about it openly and specifically, but I would say, when you asked me that question, it was the first thing that came to mind. I'm built in a way whereby I can read people; I can read rooms. I think one of my few skills is that I'm able to anticipate the next few steps in an equation. That allows me to sort of work backwards from there to say, OK, so I'm sitting here, and this is what this person's saying to me. This is where this is going to lead. Do I want it to go there or there, or there or there? How do I work backwards from that to make sure it lands where I want it to land. When I say that it's not a case of manipulation or being calculated, it's more, how do I get the best outcome for the people in this room today?

Likewise for Gavin Tollman of TTC:

The thing I'm most proud of is the nation that I came from. If you asked me to describe South Africans in a singular word, I'll say it is 'resilient'. And the ability to move into whatever gets thrown at you. I was a white, young man growing up at a time of apartheid. And yet all our family knew it was wrong. We approached things very differently, out of step with the rest of the nation. So, we are always ready to do what we think is right. And I guess if you said to us, what was the wiring? It really was one of not focusing on the things out of our control but more so the things that we can influence. The things that we could make an impact with. Our belief has always been: don't try and fix everything. Apply your focus, your energy, to making a difference in your little playing field. And if everyone does the same, you get the great, greater benefit of the good.

Other leaders were involved in the tragedy of others, which was the case for Darrell Wade of Intrepid:

It was 2003 so the company was about thirteen, fourteen years old. And we lost a fourteen-year-old girl in Borneo. We were taking the family up a mountain, Kinabula. The two kids of the family had kind of not followed instructions. They left the trail, and they got lost in the fog at around 13,100 feet (4,000 m). And long story short, we found the boy in, I don't know, fifteen hours or something. After six days we found the girl dead. That was the first death we'd ever had as a business.

I got on a plane only about six hours after she went missing. Both kids were still missing at that point. By the time I arrived in Borneo the son had been found, but the girl was still missing. And so, I lived with the family for the next five days until we found the body. And it was just the most horrendous time I've ever had. It really grounded me on the issue of health and safety, just because I saw the pain that family was going through and to a certain extent I was going through as well.

I came back and changed everything in the company in terms of safety. We'd never taken safety seriously. We had to employ people who knew what they were doing. We had to put procedures in place. Whilst the father was incredible, he said that Ellie's death was her fault, and his fault as the father because he was with them. I kind of thought it was not right because we were the ones who knew the mountain. We were the ones who had the duty of care where they should have been taken care of. We should never have let that happen. I used to believe in accidents, now I don't believe in accidents – accidents are just circumstances that haven't been managed well and haven't been predicted well.

Or, as in the case of Dan Richards, of Global Rescue, it was a tragedy they were forced to face:

I try to live every day meaningfully. I almost died in my sophomore year in college, rupturing my spleen on the football field. I was bleeding to death on the field. It's given me a different perspective on life and how fragile it is and how important every day is. But also, if you really set your mind to something, and I did in terms of recovering, you can get knocked down and nearly die and still come back. I played two more years and did very, very well. So, that was confirmation to me that I was up to the challenge.

Whatever the case, whether a crisis happened around them, to them or both, with crisis comes focus, for one and for all, as reinforced by Alan Winde, premier of the Western Cape:

Lots of things prepare you for this. Although, I mean, nothing can really prepare you for the big thing, and it is the biggest thing that I've ever had to manage in my life, but if I reflect, there are so many other things that happen along the way that in their little way prepare you. So, I mean, I think here in the Western Cape 'Day Zero' water crisis was in a way a very big learning curve and a preparation, how we managed that there was a disaster coming our way. We knew it was coming. We had to do a whole lot of things. It was an event that we weren't going to fail on. Everybody had a focus.

WIRED BY A SIGNATURE WORK CHALLENGE

For some leaders, their wiring goes back to their professional roots. Aviation leaders Willie Walsh of IATA and Paul Griffiths of DAA are clear in this regard. Willie recalls the time vividly:

I got thrown into the role of CEO at Lingus post 9/11. I was appointed on the 19th of October, which turned out to be a Friday. So, from post 9/11, I was in my role as COO. Then it was very much into survival mode. But then Lingus needed to appoint a CEO because we didn't have one at the time and nobody wanted it. I've been pretty clear about that. Nobody wanted the job. So, when the chairman approached me and said, 'Look, we think you're the best person for the job,' I said, OK. And he said, 'Do you want to think about it?' I said, 'No, nothing to think about. Somebody has to do it. I'm happy to do it.' And he said, 'But have you thought about the consequences? If this goes wrong, what's that going to mean for you?' And I said, 'Yeah, but if it goes right, it's going to be fantastic.'

Paul Griffiths of DAA has a similar revelation:

I've got a computer science and music background, a strange combination. But of course, everyone knows now that music and computer science and maths and physics and all those things all come together and with music, you've got a sense of artistry as well. Working for [Sir Richard] Branson, I had to use all my skills because he was a visionary, he wasn't a conventional mind at all. And I used to wonder how his brain works sometimes because he'd come with these incredible ideas. And he was so determined to make them succeed, even when they didn't, because it was

*the three that succeeded against the twenty that failed that got him to where
he is today. And he was so determined with the airline to make it work.
And I felt that I had the ability to sort of make his dreams reality, because
I had an empathy with the creative side. I also had this idea of creating a
vision of what good might look like for Virgin Atlantic. He and I really
hit it off. And he got me very, very involved in the growth of the airline. I
spent thirteen amazing years working for him, fighting as David against
Goliath, and doing some pretty incredible things during that period that
were audacious and confident and bold, very countercultural. And we
were, we were pirates. We were more pirates than pioneers. I think that
really drove me. Every single situation I've been in since then, it's been
a transformational situation where I've been brought in to make, to be a
disruptor, to make things better. And I think if you are never satisfied with
the status quo, and you can always see ways of improving things that
leads to a very dynamic and hopefully infectious way.*

WIRED WHILE GROWING UP

In a similar way to professional training, some leaders had their wiring set
through a hobby when they were young. As a competitive athlete growing
up, Kimarli Fernando of Sri Lanka's tourism board always saw through
to a win:

*I swam for Sri Lanka. I was told you can't swim six miles. Women don't
swim six miles in Sri Lanka. You can't swim six miles. And I said, but I
trained with all the guys. I do the same training. Why can't I do it?*

As a boy scout, Fred Dixon of NYC Tourism + Conventions always saw
the details necessary to be prepared:

*I do think about this from time to time and I give a lot of credit to my
mother. I grew up in a scouting family. I'm an eagle scout. You know, my
sister was in scouting. Both of my parents were. And so much of scouting
is about being prepared, right? And my mom used to drill me when we were
kids and we would get in the car, even if we were going to get groceries or
if we were going on a longer trip, she would ask me to pay attention on
the way there. And I had to navigate her on the way back. She always
ingrained in me this sense of independence, of leadership, this sense of
being prepared to step into the lurch at any moment. And that's who she*

is. And that's how she operates. She is a 'get it done' gal from the word go. She's a true leader in every way. She can make a decision in a heartbeat. And she's a real inspiration for me. And so, I think as a young child, one, I think I take that from her, but two, I think it also prepared me. It put me on this path of, in a sense, service to others, which is really what a lot of my career has been about.

As a young class leader, Brad Dean of Discover Puerto Rico soon felt the weight and honour of being the one people turned to:

I was seven or eight years old. I can't remember the exact age. I was in the second grade at Maple elementary school in the middle of nowhere in central Illinois. My teacher was an absolute saint, her name was Mrs Holmes. It was the first or second week of school and each week she would appoint a class leader. Now let me tell you, second grade, Mrs Holmes, when she tapped you to be the class leader, this was big stuff. I mean, this was a couple of steps away from being president or prime minister, right? I mean, this was a big deal, and I took it so seriously. And I remember she came down, she got down on her knees, she leaned over the desk and she, sort of in a very hushed tone said, 'Brad, next week you will be the class leader. Here's your responsibilities.' Very serious. And I was equally serious, and I remember reading the list and studying it. And then I went up to her desk during our recess and I said, 'Mrs Holmes, what exactly is a leader?' And I'll never forget this. She naturally looked me in the eye and said, 'A leader makes everybody around them better.' That was her definition of leadership. And it kind of stuck with me. I was branded to understand that leadership wasn't about telling other people what to do, leadership wasn't about being in charge or being important. Your job as a leader was simply to make people better. And as simple as that sounds, it just always stuck with me.

As a son in a family of national service members, Dan Richards of Global Rescue always hoped to be there when others were in need:

I was raised on the Arthurian Legends. I guess as a kid, I wanted to be one of those guys that went out and charged off to do something meaningful, and to have an adventure as part of it. My father, in addition to being a real estate entrepreneur, was a Marine. My grandfather served and fought in the Pacific. My great uncle served and fought in Europe during the Second World War. Neither my younger brother nor I put on a uniform. I don't have a lot of regrets in my life, but that's one of them. I view this sort of as my mission and opportunity to serve in whatever way I can.

WIRED BY 'WHAT IF?'

As mentioned previously, leaders interviewed were well versed in discussions and debates about navigating through times of crisis. Many had done literally hundreds of interviews by the time they sat down to speak with me. But this project, these interviews proved to be different. While within a professional context, all leaders spoke with remarkable honesty and humility, taking the time shared very personally. Often it felt as though they knew this time it would be different – this time they could say more. This became clear when, in sharing their stories, they started to understand what moments in their past had set their wiring, and how that wiring has helped them as leaders to face any challenge. In all cases, their revelations were deeply thoughtful, and at times, almost confessional; for example, Darrell Wade of Intrepid said:

Was I fearful? What is fear? I think of the base thing: fear is a thing around your own personal health and safety – you or your immediate family. So, you go from that inner circle of your wife and kids, if you like, through to your extended family, through to your friends. And to be honest, I wasn't that worried about that. I kind of thought, 'Well that's for another day or who knows.' It was more around the health and financial well-being of our staff all over the place. And then the physical health of our travellers. So, I'm not sure fear is the right word. Obviously, a huge concern. I'd never been through anything like that. You're conscious of the primary safety issue for others as a tour operator. It's pretty close to the bone. You've got people in the field and you've got a duty of care over them at its most basic form. Your first duty is just that. And it's just innate.

Puneet Chhatwal of IHCL said:

I was never afraid, actually. I travelled throughout COVID and I said, maybe I'm a risk taker. I do things differently. I was not worried. Had someone told me it would take two years, maybe I would have given up. We had no clue this will keep going on. The professional focus was how to keep everything going, how to help all associates, the company, and how to reduce the losses. I mean, how to manage the losses. The losses will be there, but it's a question of the magnitude of the loss. That was the professional challenge, but how long this would be, what to keep, what not to open, how much to open, when to open even if the government allowed. So, we were one of the rare companies that stayed open. We didn't shut down even though shutting down was cheaper. So, we felt that was right. I did not fear anything either. Neither COVID nor the impact of it. I felt frustrated. It's like snakes and ladders, and you all fall and start at point zero.

Dan Richards of Global Rescue discussed fear:

I've got to be honest. I'm not sure I was ever really fearful. You know, as a student of history, I've found this whole experience to be fascinating in a weirdly detached sort of way. I've always been fascinated by how human beings behave under stress and during extraordinary times. I'd like to think about, for instance, during the Second World War, how would I have behaved? What kind of role would I have played? And it's not just then, it's in other periods of history that I've studied. So, in a weird way, I've sort of felt like this is our moment to do what we were sort of made to do. Maybe that sounds a little bit strange, but I felt like I've been up to pretty much every challenge that's been thrown at me in my life. So, I have a high degree of confidence going into challenging situations that I'm going to figure out how to unlock the way forward in the best way possible. And if I can't, then perhaps it's not doable, but that's out of my control.

Whether previously aware of their wiring or not, all the leaders recognised it was a blessing. They see it as a strength, a source of capability and possibility. They see it as a critical part of their identity. Most importantly, they see it as a gift – a calling that they must continue to safeguard lives.

CHAPTER 8

BUILDING FIREWALLS:
PROTECTING OTHERS IN TIMES OF CRISIS

What came from me was one voice.
One statement: 'I am backing your choices.'

FAHD HAMIDADDIN, CEO, SAUDI TOURISM AUTHORITY (STA)

What insights have we gained about the mindset and motivations of those who felt called to lead during a crisis? How were they able to access inner resources to step into a leadership position with confidence, clarity and courage?

One of the most important aspects of the leaders' ability to mobilise themselves as well as others towards a place of calm and control was that, at a macro level, they established what success looked like, understanding what the situation needed of them. Central to this was rapidly:

- establishing what could be brought into control in the short term and long term
- prioritising what immediate actions needed to be taken by them
- establishing an inner circle to help them work towards success

In so doing they were able to find their way to the eye of the storm and get through to the other side, all with a degree of confidence that there they would find a rainbow.

At a micro level, however, the leaders also needed to understand what others needed of them. But how do we assess the needs of others to best support them? How far can we go in our care for those caught in crisis, and importantly, how close can we get?

This can become a very distinct grey area – an area of caution where we need to be careful of how close we get especially to others within our professional worlds – people in the workplace, people with whom we have organogram-based lines of relationship. In uncertain times, how can we take on the grey areas with any degree of certainty?

GETTING COMFORTABLE IN THE GREY AREA

Within a normal, stable, business-as-usual working environment, natural lines are drawn between the professional and the personal. Crossing that line can lead to not only conflict, but conflicts of interest, which is why as a business leader, and on a day-to-day basis, it is best to keep things black and white. And so, most leaders naturally default to a job description or a role to define their strategy.

But in a crisis emotions may emerge that go beyond what would normally be deemed acceptable in the workplace. Feelings of fear, confusion, anxiety, aloneness, anger, being overwhelmed, and so many more can dramatically alter our behaviour. It is completely natural; however, it can cause us to act unnaturally with people who are used to seeing us (and us them) in a more careful and consistent package of personal branding and behaviour. Crisis-triggered emotional responses can and do reveal certain colours in our personality that we may rather keep safely tucked away at home, especially those colours that are weaker and/or darker than we usually show. Once they are out there, they are out there, and they need to be recognised as a part of who we are in the moment.

These extreme displays of emotion reflect the state of mind of those being led, and they are invaluable as the informal writing on the wall indicating what a person is experiencing. Avoiding this grey area between the professional and personal realms would be difficult and damaging to the person suffering. For this reason leaders need to show empathy and compassion, rapidly assessing not only how those around them are behaving, but how they are *feeling* – what they were truly *needing*.

As the leaders in this book explain, this assessment had to be done sensitively, respectfully, personally and repeatedly. This is especially important as the crisis continues to grow in reach, building the momentum of risk, and showing few signs of mercy.

THE NEEDS OF THOSE BEING LED

In interview after interview, with leader after leader, it became vividly clear what the people around them needed. Those around them needed leadership. Honest leadership. Leadership that recognised them as human, not simply staff. And leadership that was based not only on what people *heard* and understood, but what they *saw*.

Clear themes rapidly emerged through our conversations – themes that offer a valuable point of reference for when we are called on to lead, as well as when we are calling on others to lead.

VISIBLE LEADERSHIP

People matter, presence matters, symbols matter. The ongoing presence of leaders, no matter how tired, frustrated, concerned or overworked and overwhelmed they were, was a non-negotiable.

> *Everyone needed a symbol of strength and confidence,*
> *and that became the leaders that they trusted.*
> *They needed to see and hear their leaders being real*
> *and showing empathy and humanity.*

Staff also needed to be heard by their leaders, not just as professionals (in government or in business) but as individuals. This aspect of leadership during a crisis was taken very seriously by all leaders profiled; for instance, Dan Richards of Global Rescue explained:

> *As the CEO and leader of an organisation, I would never ask anything*
> *of my people that I wouldn't be willing to do myself. If I can't muster*
> *the courage to do what's needed, then I can't expect them to. At the end of*
> *the day there are going to be those who have to respond. Who do we look*
> *to in society to respond? I am one of those people, even before I started*
> *Global Rescue. If there is something terrible happening in front of me, to*
> *somebody that needs help, I'm going to do what I need to do, at the risk of*
> *myself to try and make things better for that person. I'm capable, I'm able.*
> *It's my responsibility.*

The discomfort of having to step forward and finding the words to help their people find a light in the darkness was clear. But they knew that hiding was not an option. As Puneet Chhatwal of IHCL said:

> *How do you respond to your own people? Do you sit hiding in your flat?*
> *Do you not go out to the hotels where all these people are expected to work?*
> *You had to go out and you had to go show your face. That was important.*

Paul Griffiths of DAA revealed:

> *We had no playbook, we had no script, in most cases we didn't even have any information. I think it was a combination of having to be bold in the face of adversity, because you knew that the very bad leaders would just sit on their hands and do nothing. Indeed, some of the most frustrating things that have happened is where people say I don't have the jurisdiction to decide, or that isn't up to us, or I'll have to wait for a decision from someone else. That's not my style. I'd rather exceed my authority, and fortunately here in the UAE, I have a greater level of authority than I've ever had in any other position. But I also feel that I can test the boundaries of that authority.*

They continued to display their leadership, even during their weakest moments, as Alan Winde, premier of the Western Cape, recalled:

> *Remember that in the middle of all this I contracted COVID myself. That was interesting, having to deal with this, where the doctors were telling you they're going to book you into the hospital. I said, but the hospital's 200 metres away and I've got a province to run. I can't do that. One hour on a Zoom call and I would be wiped out and then have to sort of cover, because I couldn't have people see me wiped out. Another hour later, I had to be back on the next call. Everybody was petrified of what was going on. You couldn't allow anybody to see that you were also worried about what was happening. It's hard to remember because I knew that I didn't feel so good, but I also knew I couldn't show weakness in that time. I had to make sure that our citizens remained strong, even more so than our team because everybody was scared. I think I just tried not to show too many people too much. I tried not to be too vulnerable and then I was there as much as I could be, logged on and zoomed and teamed, as much as I could be.*

CLEAR COMMUNICATION

At the heart of this ability to find the eye of the storm is establishing information that is going to be helpful and separating that from information that is going to be hurtful.

> *At the beginning there was a world of information swirling around. There was so much information emerging, and changing so rapidly, that it became unnerving and unhealthy.*

During an unfolding crisis it can be so difficult to grab hold of the lifeline of information. Some of the information available may be facts, however these facts may not be sufficient to enable clear, confident identification of trends. Other data may not yet be verified. Additionally, rumours may be spreading, amplified through social media. While being highly engaging at a global level this social media space can rapidly turn into an environment of extreme, excessive noise. This can be deeply unhelpful and even hurtful, at the individual level, especially when social media becomes antisocial, ill-informed, aggressively opinionated and purposefully divisive. The pandemic was not immune to such realities. As Paul Griffiths of DAA described:

> *Of course, the world did panic, and the responses were far more dramatic. I think one cannot deny that the threat to life that the COVID-19 virus presented was very significant. The other problem is on the other side, not only did we have a mass spread of panic and fear across the world, but there was also that conspiracy theory stoked by social media. I think one of the things that we learned from the pandemic is that the concept of democratic election and the concept of social order were both very, very severely challenged by the pandemic. It was very clear that the governments were not going to have an easy time being able to instruct their populations what to do. There was a very strong countercultural movement. People ignored safety measures. I think in a lot of cases, the spread of COVID-19 was made worse by the fact that people didn't do as they were told.*

This situation cost countries significant time, and credibility, as leaders were questioned about their honesty. People needed other people and nations needed other nations. Divides, however, were starting to show. From Sri Lanka, Kimarli Fernando noticed:

> *At that time, I was watching the UK and there were people who didn't believe the government, didn't believe it was happening. They didn't respect their leaders. Here, I think people believed what the government was*

> *saying. There was a lot of communication from the minister of health, the director general, every day, twice a day, giving authentic information every day, like 'do this, do that'. They had credibility.*

Nowhere was this information and credibility issue more apparent than in the media where coverage was immense, but not always helpful. Dan Richards of Global Rescue said:

> *Sensationalism across the entire spectrum of the media is the norm rather than the exception, unfortunately. We had to focus on the media we knew we could trust which meant helping my teammates figure out what's real and what's not, trying to drill down to actually get to the data that's driving the headlines, being wary of letting their emotions be ruled by [especially social media] headlines. It was really, really important.*

People needed their leaders to be honest and they needed to trust what they were hearing, the content and the source. This is natural in the best of times, but especially true when people feel in danger professionally, personally, directly or indirectly. With masses of misinformation filling social media and making the rounds as conspiracy theories, false conclusions and simply incredible rumours, consistency of information was vital to proactively embed and update what was fact, while correcting or disputing what was clearly fiction and fear.

We cannot forget, however, that this was a crisis never before seen and experienced. Those moments of trying to make sense of it all at the outset, and then realising that initial predictions (and prayers) were not to be realised, are unforgettable for many leaders.

Willie Walsh of IATA recalled:

> *It was late January, probably early February, when the bell started ringing in my head and it became obvious pretty quickly after that this was something unlike anything we had seen before. And just as everybody was at the time, I'm sure you were, we were all talking positively about it. 'It's probably going to be bad for a couple of months, then we'll get the summer in the northern hemisphere. This will be like the normal sort of seasonal flu. The hot weather will improve things. And by the middle of summer, we should be getting back to normal.' But obviously that never happened.*

Every day, new understanding was emerging that demanded a rethink of old hypotheses, which is why leaders needed to be honest when they were misinformed, had miscommunicated, or had missed something completely. The ability of a leader to say, 'I am not sure' and even 'I was wrong' has come through as one of the strongest aspects of effective, trusted, credible leadership. Making mistakes was understandable – everyone was dancing in the dark, toes will naturally get stepped on. But with honesty, even the most dangerous of dances can be moved through. Where did leaders find themselves losing credibility and trust? When they chose to defend former, incorrect statements and continued to reinforce misunderstanding.

CONNECTION

With literally millions separated from their places of work and people of daily interaction with no sign in sight of a return to 'normal', another core need to emerge was pure and simple routine connection – ongoing engagement not only through the communication of leaders with their teams, but activity in an increasingly virtual environment where, despite the tech-disconnect, people felt stable and supported, and where momentum and productivity were visible.

> *Recognising the need for connection is what sets leaders apart. This is where leadership is a verb and they lead not only with great confidence and courage, but immense compassion.*

Marloes Knippenberg of Kerten Hospitality explained the importance of maintaining a human connection:

> *If I look back now, I wasn't afraid. I was just very focused on making sure that we would come out of it OK, and that everybody was OK. And that wasn't just the team, but also stranded guests and owners. I think being perfect is almost impossible. And so, I'd say try to do the best within your capabilities and capacities in a situation that is the first time ever, that you're not familiar with. Even if you read about crisis and crisis management and how to communicate etc., at one stage you just had to take a very human approach.*

This need to be human was common across industries, from academia to the media and tourism. Professor Demian Hodari of EHL said:

We had to understand that students had to adapt and couldn't just automatically engage for three hours online and thus we could not do things the same way as before. Our teaching, our pedagogy, had to adapt to the situation.

Rani Raad of CNN stated:

My first reaction was to reach out to those people to say, I know you're dealing with this, and now you've got that on top of it. What can I do? How can we help? What do you need? I took that and multiplied it by X hundreds of people, whether it was by virtue of town halls or direct emails. I remember in the early days I was emailing people on a regular basis. I remember that very clearly, I was sending individual emails on random days at random hours of the day, entirely randomly saying, 'Hey, how are you, Joel?', 'How are you Misaki? How are things in Tokyo?' Nothing else. Like there was no 'What's happening with this deal or that deal?' I would wake up and I would think of this one and that one and the other one. I think the outreach at the beginning was something that really helped me connect with my teams worldwide in an organic way that probably also helped them mitigate that feeling of loneliness and frustration that they would've had in dealing with COVID. Everybody had their stories. I can list them one by one, the employee whose grandmother died from COVID, the employee who couldn't see her husband because they were quarantined somewhere else. There are so many different stories up and down the ranks of people that went through very difficult moments. I think the outreach was important. Pursuant to that, I think that helped make sure that there was an organic connection with our troops. We're hundreds of people spread around a lot of geography, but we are a tight-knit family. You've seen us all work together.

Fahd Hamidaddin of STA recalled:

I remember telling my teams in Saudi and internationally, I remember giving them a message of support and comfort that whatever choice they made that would maximise their certainty of the environment they're in, I will be supportive. I told them that I will support the investment in any solution that will make them capable of contributing. I wanted them to be occupied by doing what they think they should be doing because stopping is going to simply take their attention to things that worry unnecessarily. If that's a choice they want to make, I will support, but if that's a choice they don't want to make, then I will invest in supporting a convenient platform for participation. I invested in their home offices, invested in training. For the people in Saudi, I encouraged them to be with their loved ones, go home, take care of themselves first so they can be a source of support, comfort, and assurance to those that are in need. As things became much clearer, it was a lot easier for them to engage in how we should shape our working channels better. It wasn't coming from me. It was coming from them.

Malcolm Hendry of Red Carnation Hotels reflected:

Every crisis will be different. But when I think how other people handle crises, I'd probably pay a bit more attention to specifically staff when they are coming back into the business. That can be coming back into the business tomorrow in a short-term crisis or coming back off the furlough that we saw. If there's another pandemic and we had another period of staying at home for months, I'd certainly be more aware of the pitfalls that can actually cause. The short-term openings that we did, you didn't really see it until you started bringing all our team back. You didn't see how it had changed people. But it did. I'd definitely be more aware of the effect that whatever crisis that happened could have on people coming back into your business, either short-, medium-, or long-term.

The need for connection reached even those in the crisis response community, whose business it is to take on the roughest of challenges, as Dan Richards of Global Rescue stated:

I began doing a weekly call across all of our companies and all of our geographies. And up to now, we're in the sort of waning days where I've kept doing it. We transitioned to every other weekend. We just did that until a couple of months ago, up to like 120 calls where I've got to actually get up and say something that is worth listening to. To be able to report to people and give them some level of situational awareness about what's happening, even if things are really dark, it is to be able to give them hope.

> *It wasn't just about understanding what their people needed. It was their understanding of what they needed as leaders, their own needs for connection and decompression, and their own need to not disappoint those who were trusting them.*

This concept of connection links perfectly to a central premise of *The Call to Leadership*: the belief that Mother Nature is hoping that good can, and will, emerge from this crisis. We can find light through the darkness; we can come through stronger together. At individual and collective levels across the world, the recognition of our needs started to emerge as one of the inspiring legacies from the unfolding tragedy. Did leaders recognise this in themselves?

The question had to be asked, and so I did:

WHY ARE YOU A BETTER LEADER BECAUSE OF COVID?

Unsurprisingly, leaders admitted that they now see themselves as better leaders because for the first time in their leadership careers, they had to become personal. The pandemic was just lasting too long for them to hold their breath until it was 'over'. The sustained crisis pushed their own emotions and needs to the back. They had to be emotional with others with whom they normally maintained a very formal front, dropping their guard, revealing themselves as human, not just as someone who is in a position at the helm.

This crisis gave them permission to think about themselves, rediscovering what mattered to them in their lives. It was the first time in a long time that leaders who were used to travelling the world all year were able to discover a world just outside their doorstep. Julia Simpson of the WTTC revealed:

> *I did a lot of walking, which was fantastic. I just walked, I found trainers, I walked miles and miles, and I loved it. I went on all these walks with big thinkers, and we'd go into graveyards at Hampstead or Kensal Rise and read the gravestones. I think there was a connection between the living and the dead. That was quite powerful, which is*

*another thing that I think the death of the Queen has evoked. Life suddenly
felt much more fragile. There was a sense of our own mortality because
one possibly could get COVID and die of it or your friends or family
could. I think also there were some real shockers that really upset me during
COVID. I think the way we treated people in care homes was horrendous,
not being able to go and visit elderly families. It wasn't my case. It was a
close friend of mine whose husband is in a care home. I mean it was cruel
beyond belief and not letting people be with their loved ones when they died
in hospital. I found those two things really hard for people.*

They were also able to discover the pleasure of reading their way into the
world of others, as Willie Walsh of IATA described:

*I started reading books, physical books rather than Kindle, again which
is probably the opposite of what you would've expected. But for some
reason I'm there and I'm looking at all of these books that I bought over
the years that I haven't read. I have lots of books on my Kindle, but I just
picked up a book and I started really enjoying that again. I'm still reading
books, every time I fly through Heathrow, I go into the bookshop there.
That's something that I appreciate, but only did because of going through
lockdown. I don't think I would've picked up a book if we hadn't gone
into lockdown the way we did.*

They were able to focus on keeping themselves healthy as well as devote
time and attention to their loved ones. Fahd Hamidaddin of STA reflected
on this period:

*I think I worked on my personal attention to myself, my relationship
with people that mattered and businesses, even government and how the
government can improve its efficiencies. I initiated several tracks, all under
one big theme. When everybody's thinking of how we can go back, what
are the things that we should never go back to? Can I tell you; my proudest
moments were when I went to the doctor and he told me throughout the
past four years, this is the healthiest I've seen you. It was a year and
a half after lockdown. I took care of myself a lot better. I so enjoyed
capturing my observations as learnings and reflecting and bouncing them
back with different soundboards, people, including the one and only Anita.
But I think I learned a lot from this experience on so many levels.*

Geoffrey Kent of A&K said:

> *What it really taught me is that I'm lucky in that I have such a beautiful family. I have these gorgeous little twins, and COVID gave me a chance to be with them. I was able to teach them how to swim and how to ride a bicycle. I had some really amazing times with them, which I've never done because I travelled 270 days a year. So, like, hello, goodbye. That's what Mother Nature really gave me, I actually told myself maybe I should start to calm down.*

Hon. Najib Balala recalled:

> *We managed to bond together with family. We built everything around our family for two months. We were actually in quarantine with family, and we missed many of our family and friends. So today I am proud that I reached out to all my members of family. We are a big family, so we care for each other.*

Malcolm Hendry of Red Carnation Hotels remembered:

> *To start with it was actually harder being at home, because I work in the hotel all the time, every day. We'd never been through a pandemic before. We've never been in a lockdown. So, I did two days (at home), and the first day didn't make sense because I was at home. There's no hotel around me so I can't go and check the boilers. Nothing really worked and it didn't make sense to my wife because she's never had me work from home. My son was confused because Daddy's at home, but he's doing things more than normal. It didn't even make sense to Dennis (the dog) because he wouldn't leave me alone. I got to day two and I thought, this is not going to work for me. Then I was coming in every day, and it made more sense. Everyone knew I was still working, and I've always worked from the hotel, so that was OK. But there were silver linings, and the silver linings were that I wasn't in the hotel until 8.30 p.m. because there were no guests to see.*

Some leaders used the time to learn more about the time they were living through, such as Fred Dixon of NYC Tourism + Conventions:

> *I learned a lot about viruses and how communicative viruses can be and how quickly they can spread. I learned not to take our health for granted*

and the importance of our health, and I think most importantly, the importance of well-being. I think the one legacy of this crisis that we're now seeing unfold in an ever-increasing way is the toll it's taken on mental health. I think that's true for everyone. I think we're going to find out that we all have some level of PTSD. I think the post-traumatic stress from this is just now showing itself. We've seen leaders in our own organisation, people who have come through the fire, who have said, I need to go in a different direction now, and that's OK because we all have to recognise that we have been through something remarkable, hopefully something that will only happen once in our life. For me, the reset coming out of that, of putting your own health and your own mental well-being above all is, I think, a gift. Something that we received with great pain and agony, but it's an important lesson.

Finally, there were leaders who simply stopped to appreciate the people who made it possible for them to get through this time. Dan Richards of Global Rescue recognised their work:

I've got to be honest. The bravery of the people around me and who I observed, the everyday bravery of the men and women driving the delivery trucks, working in the warehouses, and keeping the supply chains open and going, keeping us all fed, delivering home heating oil, and doing all the things that prevented society from completely melting down. Working those incredibly long hours sometimes without access to the needed PPE and other kinds of resources. That's extraordinary and not all of them made it through, right? A lot of them did, but some of them didn't, some of them got sick, and some of them died. I witnessed that just within our company. There were real trials happening to many of us, pretty much every day.

This open, honest, pure understanding by the leaders of themselves was so important. Similarly, leaders recognised that although they needed to focus on the people that they cared for – family and friends, employees and other colleagues, customers and guests – they also needed to care for themselves. For the first time, many understood that it is acceptable to give oxygen to parts of one's own life to become a stronger leader. As a result of the dramatic negative impact the pandemic had on lifestyle, leaders became much more engaged in their own physical and mental health, actively creating time to take care of themselves.

Uniquely, understanding needs and articulating them out loud for this project made many leaders realise not only what was needed of them for others to be strong, but what they needed of and for themselves, for their leadership to stay strong.

CHAPTER 9

THE LANGUAGE OF LEADERS:
THE CRITICAL ROLE OF COMMUNICATION

*The hierarchy was never a thing with me.
There was never any of that. I reached out to people,
people then reached out in return, and from there we just
kept in touch, and we just kept thinking about different
mechanisms that we can put in place to help people.
There was never a point where I felt like we took our foot
off the pedal. I hope that will pay dividends in loyalty,
and people recognising how much we care for them and how
much I care for people within this team that we manage.*

RANI RAAD, FORMER PRESIDENT, CNN INTERNATIONAL (COMMERCIAL)

'Please sit down. There is something I need to tell you.'

Hearing those words, even without a hint of why they are spoken, can cause our hearts to start to beat a little louder, our bodies feel a little heavier and our minds start to whirl. The radius of our world seems to pull in. So much becomes muted aside from what is about to be heard.

When there is a hint about what may be said, the beating of your heart is even louder, the muting is stronger, the body is heavier. This is a natural reaction to receiving a shock, as discussed in earlier chapters. No doubt you can relate to such a moment, such a feeling, such a reaction. A moment in our lives when we were suddenly given news that we knew would shake and shape our world like we never anticipated:

- an accident
- a diagnosis
- a company restructuring
- a massive storm system about to hit our home
- a legal document stating the end of a marriage
- the end of the life of a loved pet
- the loss of a family member
- the loss of a friend
- the loss of a dream

We have all experienced those time-stands-still moments in different ways, but the reaction to each was no different: immediate shock. When that immediate shock happens, there is only one thing that can extinguish the flames suddenly rising in our mind and heart, calming the panic setting in: information. For this reason, it is imperative that leaders be exceptional communicators, especially in a crisis when their words can become a lifeline. We saw it with the pandemic. As soon as a fresh news item broke, we all started to feel something was deeply wrong again. Many immediately turned to leaders who they felt they could trust to provide information that would guide them to best respond. Billions turned to the World Health Organization (WHO), and millions looked to their government leaders including heads of state, heads of foreign affairs and heads of ministries of health. Closer to home, we felt the people around us had the information we could trust:

- healthcare practitioners in our local community
- colleagues in our work environment who we could look to for solid information
- family and friends who we knew were good at interpreting what was happening and therefore how to respond

The ability to communicate is at the heart of a leader's ability to guide people successfully and sensitively through a storm. The leaders who could do this were visible and they were real. And yet, it is very easy to look at leaders in times of crisis and feel that they are simply talking or informing and updating. The reality is quite the contrary, particularly in times of high complexity, high anxiety, low clarity and low certainty. In the case of the pandemic, the first signs of smoke, where the smoke was coming from, how rapidly the flames would rise, how deeply they would harm, and how long they would burn was completely unknown. Never before had our shared world experienced a crisis that was:

- everywhere across the globe
- threatening the health of everyone
- causing the questioning of everything we did in our lives – how we lived, worked, played, even hugged

Also, the crisis was *invisible*, which meant it unleashed:

- fear
- fiction
- blame
- disbelief

In all cases, an immediate shock can cause our imagination to run wild. How does one possibly find the words when:

- it is so hard to find the source and spread of a crisis?
- the ability to access trustworthy information is so severely limited?
- it is unclear where, and to whom, to turn for certainty?
- rising levels of fear are having a clear impact on mental and physical stability?

Leaders who were wired to step forward needed to make sense of what was happening and find the words to help others find a sense of calm. They knew it was critical for information, communication and connection to be as strong as possible.

Fahd Hamidaddin of STA reflected:

I'm a strong believer that the source of all the negative behaviours, if I may generalise for simplicity, is fear. All the ego problems and overreactions come from a great source of fear. Fear has different forms – from fear for life to fear for ego and image. That's why I believe a level of certainty is critical. There is a natural fear in uncertainty, and when the fear is beyond what's natural, no matter what you do and what you tell them, you're not talking to what really matters to their core – a need for certainty. Start from there and once you establish that connection then you can build on it layer by layer based on different readiness and circumstances.

Throughout the crisis, our leaders instinctively found a way of communicating to lead others to a place of calm, even if they were in the eye of the storm.

But is the voice of leadership really that important? To better understand and appreciate the importance of communication, all we need to do is reflect on times of crisis in our own lives when leadership was absent and information was not readily available. When information is withheld it creates nervousness, anxiety and distrust. Like the beam of a flashlight able to break through darkness, the words of leaders provided the much-needed direction and momentum key to building confidence. With their presence, therefore, came much-needed peace. For this reason, it is fundamentally important that we understand how the language of leaders helps people find their way through a crisis.

> *When a crisis occurs, information is one of the only elements that can stop the escalation of our thoughts, emotions and fears. Information can put things into perspective.*

Information can put us at ease, as at the very least it may warn us of something happening that demands our immediate attention, giving us an indicator of how strongly, swiftly and seriously we need to respond. This is where the language of leaders matters most. It is not just about *what* is said, it is about *how* it is said, *when, where* and by *whom*.

THE PATH TO THE EYE OF THE STORM

Effective communication is essential for successful leadership during a crisis – and success in being led. In a crisis, communication is not merely an administrative task for leaders to fulfil. It is an essential part of leading. Why? Just think about yourself and how you have responded in the past when a crisis has hit.

As we have seen, when 'the moment' occurs, our response is primal and our first priority is looking for safety. How 'safety' is defined differs depending on the situation and the shock. As an example: you learn of your business shutting down, and therefore your employment ending. What is 'safety'? In the immediate term, safety means:

- your ability to continue to earn money
- your ability to get another job
- your ability to take care of your loved ones

Beyond the short term, safety means:

- your ability to maintain your home and lifestyle
- your ability to protect your savings
- your ability to protect your career path

Here is another example: you learn you have a serious illness that demands immediate levels of care. What is 'safety'? In the immediate term, safety means:

- your ability to get, and afford, medical help, to stay alive
- your ability to stop everything else in your life, especially working,

to give yourself the time and focus needed

- your ability to protect others closest to you from fear while getting the care you need

In the long term, safety means:

- your ability to protect your job
- your ability to protect your future finances
- your ability to envision your future hopes and see them come to fruition

Even in these two examples you can feel the impatient, desperate hunger for information you can trust. Which is exactly why leaders must, absolutely must, communicate during a crisis. Do we really understand why? Let's take a closer look, and as we do, think about it from your own, personal perspective. But do not think about this need for information in your 'here and now' when your thoughts are calm and collected, think about it in the context of a time when you were alerted to a crisis that unleashed chaos in your world.

CONTROL

What did leaders around you need to do in a crisis? First and foremost, they established control. When a crisis occurs, leaders must embed an understanding of the *what*, communicating clearly in order to provide clear context to help others immediately understand:

- what exactly is happening, as much as 'exactly' can be explained in the moment
- what can be done to protect oneself
- what to expect thereafter, as much as one can provide that direction in the moment

Through their language, leaders can have a direct influence on people's ability to understand:

- what is happening to them
- how they can take control of their own emotions and reaction
- how they can eliminate risk to themselves (physically, emotionally, financially, professionally, whatever the case may be in that situation)

In addition, leaders need to keep communication lines strong to mobilise the individual and collective action needed to ensure their people safely, calmly and confidently get through the crisis. Leaders need to navigate others through their own *fight, flight* or *freeze* responses which, if not managed, can make a crisis worse. As articulated by Dan Richards of Global Rescue:

> *When the world is losing its mind and people are going crazy, keeping yours is doubly important. It's hard. It's really hard.*

CREDIBILITY

Leaders also need to immediately establish their credibility. When so much is happening and there is so much distraction, leaders need to clearly demonstrate that they are the point person. They need to make it clear they are accountable and people can turn to them for protection, because they are taking responsibility for the situation and are actively working to resolve it.

> *Leaders can become the sponge for the questions, concerns, fears and even follies of others. They can contain the spread of panic, rumour and damage. They become the magnifier of clarity and courage to get through and inspire confidence.*

This behaviour is clearly conveyed by Paul Griffiths of DAA:

> *Of course I was afraid, I'm human, I'm flesh and blood. And the thing is that as a leader, if you are put in a situation like COVID-19, every person looks to you for the answers. And if you don't have the answers, you can't be a leader, but if the answers are not available, what I had to do is try and assemble an answer that I thought stood a chance of being close to the truth.*

This is where the *how* of communication is critical. Leaders who step forward and show they are not only a leader but also human embed immense confidence in the minds and hearts of their people. In a crisis, as called out earlier, a grey area emerged between the personal and professional. A leader's honesty of self, shared with others, at the right time and in the right way, builds one of the most important aspects of effective leadership: trust. Crisis situations offer little time for testing sincerity or loyalty. Leaders who consistently demonstrate their sense of duty and responsibility are able to mobilise the individual and collective towards safety, moving them through to the other side.

COMPASSION

Lastly, leaders need to show compassion. Our humanity is laid bare in a crisis. Our need for safety becomes our priority. For this reason, leaders know that they need to push past empathy, a core aspect of everyday leadership, to show compassion. This enables them to help people manage their own deep, raw, intensely real sense of vulnerability, confusion, emotions and fears. As expressed by Fahd Hamidaddin of STA:

> *The power of communication is layered, but I want to highlight one thing. I believe that there are many real physical problems that could be solved by communication. Communication can provide solutions to an actual problem when you don't have answers. The power of communication is to be consistent. You have to control the narrative because at times of fear people are looking for leadership they trust.*

It cannot be repeated enough that the language of leaders is absolutely critical in any crisis, especially in a sustained crisis. Words matter and the compassionate words of good leaders make it clear that *you* matter.

THE MESSAGE AND THE MESSENGER

In the language of leaders there are two key components: the *message*, what is said, and the *messenger*, who is saying it. First, let's look closely at the message. As the pandemic evolved, the term 'new normal' was increasingly used. But there was no 'normal' about what we were experiencing. Life demanded we look ahead to the *next* normal, and then the next, and then the next, and then the next. Similarly, and even to this day, the term 'back to normal' can be heard but going back is not something we can do.

> *Our world has changed. The way in which we understand, value and live life has changed. There is no going back. And again, there is no normal.*

The term 'building back better' also seemed to lack real meaning. If we can rebuild our industry, economy, society, and importantly our relationship with humanity and the environment, to be better, stronger and smarter than before, why wouldn't we?

We knew going into 2020 there were many issues challenging the future of our sector. We knew we needed to take a close look at these issues to make sure that the growth of the travel and tourism sector was healthy, addressing growing concerns around:

- equality
- sustainability
- inclusivity
- longevity
- responsibility
- humanity

For all the good it was doing, the industry was also negatively impacting people and places across the globe. And we knew it, the message was clear that the industry must step up and take responsibility for creating a better, stronger future of travel and tourism. The future needed to be truly sustainable in all the ways that matter, economically, socially, culturally and environmentally. For this reason, how leaders in the new world of global travel and tourism now speak and communicate is so important. The call to action is loud and clear. Now is the time to build forward better, for all. These words of our call to action mirror what the industry ultimately values and prioritises. Or not.

Just as important as the message is the messenger.

When a crisis occurs, there is nothing more powerful than the person at the top making connection to their people their top priority. The messenger sets the focus, or not. The messenger embeds the credibility of the message, or not. The messenger reinforces what is valued and prioritised, or not. Hence why, in times of crisis, consistency of leadership presence is directly linked to sustaining the confidence and commitment of those being led, even when finding the right words is immensely challenging. Otherwise, the consequences could extend beyond the immediate and visible damage.

> *To be deprived of information, to be left alone*
> *without leadership that can be trusted, is a horrible*
> *place to be. It can be terrifying.*

During a crisis, people can feel isolated and alone, which can lead to feelings of uncertainty, confusion and being overwhelmed. If there is a lack of leadership during a crisis, people may feel abandoned, unvalued and unworthy. These feelings can further exacerbate the negative impact of the crisis on individuals, making it crucial for leaders to step up and provide a sense of guidance and support.

Just as with effective communication, effective connection is never forgotten. So too is fear-stirring silence or sticking to something previously said which now is simply not true. This applies to everyone, leaders and followers, as shared by Professor Demian Hodari of EHL:

What didn't work here was that at some places in the organisation the directors said, 'OK, we found a solution, and this is the way it's going to be. And this is forever now.' The school came up with this thing of we're going to be hybrid from now on — classes will be online and in person. We're going to double the number of students; half the students will come to school on any given day, and half won't come to the campus that day but will be online. There was a strong belief that this was the future of education and for the school. And so, as faculty we were instructed to invest our time in our online teaching as this was the future, not just during the pandemic. But we as faculty were realising that, well, this is tough. And it doesn't really work like this, you're not as effective as in person. So now we acknowledge that all this work was done by the school management and by the faculty, and then once things opened up again, all this just simply seemed to go away. Many on the faculty were left wondering, 'So are we going to stick with this hybrid teaching forever or not?' But it seemed to us that the response was, 'Oh no, you misunderstood.' But it wasn't a misunderstanding. This was an example of admitting that you got it wrong.

As this experience makes clear, it was important to acknowledge the need to embrace managing a crisis in a time of rapid change. Ultimately, it is language that is one of the most powerful and purposeful tools that a leader has at their disposal to help guide their people with confidence, courage and connection.

Or not.

CHAPTER 10

BUILDING A BETTER 'AFTER':
SEEING POSSIBILITIES POST-CRISIS

I really do believe that understanding the past and being able to see a progression is one of the most powerful ways of predicting the future. And ultimately, it is not even about predicting the future. It's about creating your future.

MATTHEW UPCHURCH, CEO, VIRTUOSO

The ability to recognise a crisis as an opportunity enabled many leaders to use a time of uncertainty and fluidity to form a stronger foundation. One after the other, these leaders overtly recognised that part of their strength was a love for the challenge of creating something new, and the ability to take what exists and look for future opportunities. Some leaders knew that what once was will never be again, both the good and the bad. Gavin Tollman of TTC realised:

> One of the earliest lessons I learned in the midst of this pandemonium was with such great clarity. Everyone was asking, 'When is this going to be over?' Do you remember that? 'When do we go back to normal?' I don't know how many times I heard that. I started asking a different question: who said that the new cannot be better than the old? That became my guiding force, how I looked at myself as an individual, having the privilege of leading a great organisation, how we could reorganise our organisation to capitalise on what we saw was to come, being able to adapt. I really was fascinated by the fact that everybody speaks so much about writing the next chapter. I said, 'Let's start a whole new book!'

For this reason, leaders can still offer an energy that provides strength even in some of the toughest times, as Hon. Premier Winde, premier of the Western Cape, explained:

> When I look back there were massive negatives. There were huge issues that we faced. But if I look back on it, this is where I've got to be careful because so many people lost loved ones, so many people lost their businesses, lost jobs. We are seeing it now in the detail of those reports on mental well-being and the impact that it's going to have for years to come

on people. But despite all of that, for me personally, it was a very exciting journey because we could have things coming at us that we didn't know what to do with, and we'd sit around tables, and we'd make a plan, and we would go and do it. We would do things that I think ordinarily, if you'd said to that very same team, this is what I want us to do – convert a convention centre into a hospital in three weeks – they would all say you are crazy, it's never, ever going to be done. But that part of it for me was exciting, having all these people, finding that energy and going and doing those things. And then the other thing that was also exciting in this journey was the humanity of people and what comes out in these times of such immense pressure.

Using the collapse of everything to create a better model for moving forward unlocked not only unique new ways of doing things, but a uniquely inspiring spirit of connection and co-creation, according to Marloes Knippenberg of Kerten Hospitality:

We really used the time to consolidate and build foundations to scale. Because we were really surrounded by incredible people that boarded the team over the last two years, we didn't reduce the team. We did not replace anybody who left. And we took measures that were actually good for people to stay with us for a longer duration. I'd say the pride is that today we're stronger than ever, and that's from a private as well as from a business perspective.

Paul Griffiths of DAA stated:

If you have an airport infrastructure that's used to processing over ninety million passengers a year, and you suddenly shut down, you have pretty much all the cost base of an infrastructure serving ninety million people, but you clearly have very little of the revenue because you turned off the main revenue-generating capability of your entire operation. We had to go into a massive programme to do what we could to save money. I think this is where the way we did it was different from a lot of other entities around the world, because we took the long-term view. We knew that this was going to cause a great deal of commercial pain. It was going to be a very, very difficult period from not just a welfare perspective, but from a commercial perspective and from a financial perspective. To paraphrase Newton's third law, every reaction has an equal and opposite reaction.

Every downturn has an equal and opposite upturn. We knew that we couldn't do anything that would fundamentally damage our operation for the longer term, because we knew there would come a time where we need the people to manage the operation when it was operating at full capacity. My view was let's take the opportunity to re-engineer the shape of the entire airport structure and think differently about how we would want to run it in the future. I thought of this as an opportunity, as a great opportunity to reshape the entire travel and tourism industry.

The pandemic even unlocked unexpected ideas that have today become invaluable new revenue generators and brand builders for businesses, as Puneet Chhatwal of IHCL discovered:

What is the business opportunity in this crisis? The mental space is not empty, thinking only of all the bad things happening. We did that in terms of launching Qmin (home delivery of signature dishes from Taj, Vivanta and SeleQtions hotels), which became a big brand for us, not just when we launched it but even today. I would say it's 30% of our business. We also have new Qmin QSR, quick service restaurants. We call it 'Qminisation' – evolution of ideas and brands. We never spent any money on building a brand. It was just done on incremental costs. The kitchens were there, the cooks were there. It was a variable cost model.

Geoffrey Kent of A&K reflected:

The proudest moment was to keep an even keel without any mass layoffs. We basically kept everybody on, and everybody did their bit and helped. As we always say, we're a family and we all did our stuff. We were lucky and we entered this without debt, no private equity, so Manfredi [Lefebvre d'Ovidio, long-time colleague and close friend, now co-owner of Abercrombie & Kent] and I could make our own decisions as we went, which we did. I think that was very lucky. We came out like a cork out of a champagne bottle the minute it was over.

Over and above innovation to save the business, in some cases leaders boldly stepped forward also inspiring others to do something, if or when they were in a position to do so. Numerous acts of compassion of various scales and styles occurred across the travel and tourism ecosystem.

In early 2020, as global borders and skies closed, the aviation community helped literally millions of stranded travellers return to a safe place, and transport essential medical staff and equipment to places in need. As shared below by the Air Transport Action Group (ATAG), the commercial aviation industry's highly respected not-for-profit association representing all sectors of the global aviation ecosystem including airlines, airports, air traffic control, and manufacturers, in 2020 the airline industry activated:

- 39,200 repatriation flights for 5.4 million displaced travellers
- 46,600 special cargo flights carrying over fifteen million tonnes of cargo, mostly medical equipment

Furthermore, aviation leaders became angels of mercy as they mobilised the global aircraft network to deliver desperately needed vaccines and hope across the world. As an example, in early 2022 the online aviation source, simpleflying.com, reported that:

> *Emirates SkyCargo has reached a tremendous milestone of transporting more than one billion doses of COVID-19 vaccines across its fleet of aircraft. This historic feat was achieved within a relatively short span of eighteen months since the first shipment of vaccines was trialled in October 2020. . . The air cargo carrier has transported more than 4,200 tonnes of COVID-19 vaccines – an equivalent of over one billion doses. These vaccines have been moved to over eighty destinations on over 2,000 Emirates flights, with close to two-thirds of the one billion doses transported to developing countries.[5]*

But the travel and tourism industry's support did not stop there. The hospitality community also played a critical role, transforming hotels and resorts into safe havens for people grounded, quarantined or needing a more liveable lockdown location. At the forefront of the thoughts of many leaders are not only citizens – guests, staff and locals – but the essential, invaluable, heroic frontline community, as beautifully demonstrated by the Taj Public Service Welfare Trust (TPSWT). The trust was established by IHCL, and the CEO and Managing Director, Puneet Chhatwal, described their work:

> *There was not one response. It was a set of responses. Number one was to help the medical fraternity, the frontline workers. The idea came through a*

friend who was a celebrity chef and the face of Indian cuisine across the world. He called me and asked if we could do something together. That's chef Sanjiv Kapoor, we are class fellows and friends for forty-one years. So, I said, 'OK, we'll do it, but what will we do?' He said, 'Once we start doing, everyone else will follow.' We started from one hospital, it went on to thirteen in various parts of the metros, which was followed by hosting medical staff.

I would say the second response is in hotels, because frontliners were not welcome at home. Especially in the high-rise Mumbai buildings, there was such a scare that people were not welcome. They could not travel anyways. They could not commute. Trains, buses, everything was shut. Somebody had to work and those people who were working, they had to go and eat somewhere or sleep somewhere. The start-up cost was higher, but it kept coming down with the volume because we had to start our flight kitchen. All the kitchens were open for very few meals in the beginning, 250 a day and it went up to 40,000 meals a day.

The third was obviously the safety of our associates.

Whether you call it peer pressure, or you call it inspirational, or you call it a good example, all other hotel groups followed.

The possibility of there not only being an 'after', but the potential of 'after' being better than before, became fuel for creativity, generosity and legacy for leaders to see signs of a rainbow while caught in the thick of the storm.

CHAPTER 11

THE HARDEST PART:
WHAT LEADERS RARELY REVEAL

For six months I didn't sleep. My brain was working.
I was thinking beyond my portfolio. I was thinking on behalf
of the president who had the responsibility of addressing issues
of the country, it's not about tourism. It's about human beings
surviving and building an economy or building a nation that
is defended against a war that we don't know.
And the war is not about military and armoury. It's about
health. That war is much more difficult to address. And my
mind was actually on fire.

HON. NAJIB BALALA, FORMER MINISTER OF TOURISM AND WILDLIFE FOR KENYA

'How are you?'

These three words are what people need to hear from their leaders when they are in a crisis, feeling pressure, panic and even pain. These three words show that a leader cares. But what about the leaders themselves? What about the pressure, panic and pain they may feel?

When leaders were asked about the personal challenges they faced while leading through the crisis, three truths emerged that exposed often overlooked aspects of leadership.

1: A CRISIS DEFINING OUR GENERATION

For many leaders, one of the hardest parts of leading during this tragic time was their recognition of the scale and severity of what was happening to us as a global community.

> *The crisis was so far beyond our industry,*
> *our community, our country, our health, our year.*
> *It was a humanitarian crisis, and it was shaping*
> *how the world looked at itself for generations to come.*

This was particularly painful when it came to recognising the impact the pandemic was going to have on children who were:

- forced into lockdowns that kept them away from their friends, families and the people who they loved, and they needed to feel love from
- facing a world without smiles as masks removed all facial expression aside from what could be communicated through our eyes

- blocked from the comfort of human touch because of social distancing, ironically at a time when so much comfort was needed
- living in the boundaries of bubbles that limited who, when and where people could come together when regulations eased, blocking little ones from the ability to play together, learn together, and enjoy spontaneous moments together
- home-schooling, dropping the baseline of their learning, and learning together, with direct care, direct education, direct support and direct reassurance of growth

All of this was going to be severe, as Rani Raad of CNN explained that one of the hardest moments of the crisis for him was when he had to tell his children why they were having to shut down the world:

> *The watershed 'a-ha' moment I felt as an individual? I need to think about what that means. It was when I had to explain it to my kids. It was the resentment that I had to do that. I was so angry, I remember, but also so thoughtful in every word I chose. There was such deep anger inside that. Why does she have to go through this? The last time this happened was a hundred years ago, like why couldn't we have waited another hundred years?*

2: LEADERS FAILING TO LEAD

Through our interviews, leaders were open in their expressions of disappointment and even anger when colleagues around them, especially those in formal leadership positions, simply stepped away. How could they make such a choice when it was their job and responsibility to step up? No doubt they had their reasons. In the moment, however, leaders interviewed struggled when recalling observing an absence of leadership. Paul Griffiths of DAA said:

> *One of the things I was most frustrated about was the fact that this was a perfect time for governments to be able to pull together, to come up with common standards, to agree protocols for travel, and to be able to make a systematic and coordinated response, to protect both the health of the general public and to protect the livelihoods and employment of industries across the world. That to me is the biggest single disappointment, that the weakness and lack of coordination and lack of desire to corroborate and*

collaborate was just absolutely visible from the word go. And I remember on conference calls where people were being terribly deferential and terribly respectful, I'd sort of weighed in and said, I just don't understand what the strategy is. There's no escape plan from the pandemic. How on earth can you sit on a call and say, 'This is not my responsibility.' You need to get out there and agree with whoever has got the power to make these decisions, to draw it all together and come up with a plan. We cannot afford to sit and wait.

Gavin Tollman of TTC stated:

One of my greatest disappointments coming out of the pandemic was the politicisation. In those initial stages humanity really did come together. We all worked collaboratively as one. I did at that moment feel fear, but I also felt optimism. But sadly, how quickly that has been forgotten.

Professor Demian Hodari of EHL reinforced the frustration, and quite honestly, disappointment, felt when those counted on to lead seemed to leave:

No one ever reached out and asked, 'How are you?' to anybody. That was a big thing in the faculty. No one checked if students and even faculty needed anything. It was just a lot of, 'Guys, there were a lot of rules and procedures to follow.' And I think that was something I learned. I felt responsible for the well-being of my students. This was a time to be more human and less rigid. That was a missed opportunity on this end. I think it left a lot of people disengaged at that point.

To see other leaders creating separation at a time when unity was needed, stepping out when they should have stepped up, and even becoming political, was heartbreaking for many of the leaders profiled. And it was distracting from what, and who, mattered in those moments when a clear call to action could be heard. Today, it is impossible for our leaders to not look differently at those who failed to respond to the call to lead.

3: THE PAIN OF PARTING

Of all the personal pains experienced by leaders, one of the most deeply penetrating was being forced to say goodbye. How do you let go of people you have worked with, admired, cared for and championed because the world shut down? How do you find the words to explain that there is no other choice? As time passed and the grounding of travel and tourism put increasing pressure on business survival, leaders were acutely aware of the implications of the crisis. They knew what the risks were, not only to human life, but to operations. Paul Griffiths of DAA said:

> *The initial very tough lockdown and the very strong messaging about masks and quarantine and working from home was I think very well placed by the UAE government here. Probably not enforceable in other jurisdictions. But I think this, followed by the early adoption of a pro-vaccine strategy, really helped open up Dubai much earlier than other countries. And I think we were equal to Israel in being able to get to the number one country where pretty much all of the population was vaccinated, this enabled us to emerge earlier from the pandemic. But I think the moments during the early stages of the pandemic, where it really illustrated how difficult this was, was in May 2020 when during the entire month of May, the same number of passengers passed through DXB as had passed through in only four hours in May 2019. So, you can see the dramatic impact on infrastructure.*

Gavin Tollman of TTC observed:

> *In that instant, the most pressing need was what did we need to do for our guests? How do we get people home? I haven't thought about this in a while. People were just getting stranded. Airlines were stopping taking people. We had thousands of people all over the world. 'How are we going to repatriate people who are everywhere?' was one of our core considerations.*

Cyril Ranque of Expedia articulates with rawness how the pain of parting was not purely all of the people that made up the business, but the performance of the business that kept the people of the business safe, secure and future-focused:

> *We had hundreds of millions of dollars going out the door every day. I think at some point we were literally fifteen days to three weeks close to bankruptcy.*

I cannot even imagine the extent of the pressure that leaders faced when they realised that the right thing to do left so many of the people they cared for feeling even less secure and hopeful. Especially in such a social industry as travel and tourism that naturally attracts young people and extroverts because they love meeting new people, discovering new places, connecting with the big wide world around them. But the world was shut down with little indication of when it would finally open again. And even when it did reopen, when would travel return? When would travellers return?

Rewinding to that time, in their 'right here, right now', very difficult decisions needed to be made. Even when it was temporary, letting people go, even if it was simply asking them to stay home from work, potentially had consequences. Leaders knew their people were at risk of periods of depression and anxiety being left alone, forced to stay apart, especially the younger, more sociable ones who are the front line of service in our industry.

On top of that, there were leaders who suffered having to let go of some of their leadership team, all victims of circumstance, the fallout of an industry shutting down because the world was unable to move, was unable to connect, was unable to travel. This was a severe cause of trauma and while leaders were making these hard decisions professionally, they were taking them very, very personally. Willie Walsh of IATA explained:

We were brutally honest with people, and it was tough, standing in front of your friends saying, 'By the way, guys, I'm sorry, but you have no job.' I wouldn't say it's a defining moment, but it's certainly reinforced in my mind that to be an effective leader, you've got to be honest, you've got to be decisive. You have to be determined. You have to have an idea as to where it is you want to go, you have to try and bring people with you, but ultimately, if a decision has to be taken, you have to take it and you can't be afraid to take it.

Darrell Wade of Intrepid stated:

We had an incredibly painful initial period. So, we made that call and then after two to three weeks, we realised we weren't going to be shutting operations for a month or whatever. We were going to be shutting operations for maybe six months, maybe twelve months. We didn't really know at that time, but we also knew that at our current burn rate, we had perhaps twelve months of cash in the bank. So, we thought, if it lasts for two years we can't last two years, so we're going to have redundancies. After a month or so we thought, OK, let's do one round of redundancies. There was incredible pain that we as a company have never experienced before, you are making extremely good people who have done nothing wrong redundant. A lot of our team, the people making others redundant, are doing something that's pretty bloody awful. That's to say nothing of the people who are being made redundant. There was a lot of survivor guilt. Really you were looking at a form of trauma, even though it was different, but there's pain going on there. Those people who'd had more counselling on that in the past worked with the team with those survivors, reinforcing, 'Hey, we're here. We're going to be OK. You did what you had to do. This is not your fault.'

Paul Griffiths of DAA explained the importance of decisive action:

Sometimes in the last two years, I've had to be far more coercive. I've had to say, I know this won't appeal to all of you, but we are going to have to do this. It's going to be painful. I'm going to have to ask you to go and have some very painful conversations with people. And you will have to insist that we get this as an outcome. And people found that uncomfortable. But I think now with hindsight, they can see for the most part, those situations have turned out the better for the decisions we made. Sometimes making a decision, even if it's not the right decision, can be the best thing you do because indecision is the thing that I think destroys people more than anything else. That feeling of rudderless behaviour, the idea that you don't know where you're going, your boss doesn't know what they're doing. You don't have the confidence to move forward. If there is no decision, that's the most debilitating position to be in.

Cyril Ranque of Expedia stated:

We're not set up to have a model where cash goes out the window so fast. And then we implemented a cost-saving program, which was obviously painful but necessary and as much as possible to avoid massive layoffs. And I know in the industry, a lot of companies went all out in laying off people. And they're now having a tonne of issues, rehiring those same people. So, we tried to be balanced in that approach so that we sized the company for future states, not just for the crisis. Otherwise, we would've fired pretty much everybody.

Dan Richards of Global Rescue described leadership decisions:

I don't know the people, but their stories are compelling to me, and I care about them. It doesn't have the same kind of impact when we're making decisions. It's a little bit like a doctor in an emergency department, right? They deal with tragedy or potential tragedy in front of them literally every single day, and the way that they have to make decisions is very clinical. And that's how we have to conduct ourselves. Always in a little bit of a detached way. I'm not as close to the day-to-day as I was when we were a much smaller and younger company, but I do get involved. It's a different story when you're dealing with people who you care about, who you work with every day. Some of the folks that I work with, we've worked together for more than a decade, and to see them and their families dealing with COVID, getting sick and trying to figure out how best to support them. And yet still being able to carry on doing what you're supposed to be doing every day, dealing with the emotional impact of that. It was draining in a way that was unexpected.

As difficult as these defining moments were, many who inspired strength, trust and hope as leaders were recognised to be making decisions for the greater good, with clarity, confidence and consistency.

> *The pain leaders felt making the hardest decisions was visible. The pressure leaders were experiencing to keep businesses alive was visible. Their humanity was visible. And for this reason, the sympathy of others was possible.*

One aspect of the crisis, which often people forget about, was recognising that leaders had their own fears, they were human. Leaders also fell seriously ill. Leaders also lost loved ones. Leaders were also looking for signs of confidence and reassurance. Leaders were also suffering and questioning whether they would make it through, but they had to do this in silence.

Yet, leaders knew that when it came to being public facing, they needed to be strong, they needed to be consistent, they needed to be courageous. At the same time, they needed to be compassionate in a way that helped people face, not increase, fears. Hon. Premier Winde, premier of the

Western Cape said:

> *I couldn't sleep. I mean, I'd get to bed at whatever time and within an*
> *hour I was awake again. I can't tell you how many times I'd be sitting*
> *at my desk, researching, reading, looking at the data, questioning, yeah, it*
> *was tough, because we didn't know. Remember, at that stage we were still*
> *in our tourism season, it was the high season. We were buzzing and doing*
> *very, very well. It wasn't in the southern hemisphere. We were quite happy,*
> *although behind the scenes we were all very anxious.*

Kimarli Fernando expressed this fear for others and her determination to
maintain tourism in Sri Lanka:

> *I was afraid for the world. I was afraid and concerned for the people when*
> *we saw things. I was afraid for the world, but I felt that we will overcome*
> *it. When I saw people in India and Italy, I sat and cried for the world.*
> *I have cried for the world, the suffering. The inner peace is because it*
> *[keeping tourism alive] is a cause for the people, it's for the people. It's for*
> *my people, I felt it's my responsibility. I would not have given up.*

Part of this challenge was a leader's ability to control their own imagination
and concerns. As hard as these times were for leaders, despite being as
accessible, supportive and empathetic as possible, many leaders were seen
as uncaring and unreasonable, making hard decisions. This demanded
high leadership performance when sentiment, mood and confidence
were so low. There was a sense of pride among some individuals in their
ability to be uncompromising and push through difficult situations, even
if it meant asking for forgiveness later. They saw it as a sign of strength
and were confident in their ability to motivate others to persevere. For
example, Willie Walsh of IATA said:

> *I always say I was inspired by George Bernard Shaw's quote about*
> *the reasonable man: the reasonable man adapts himself to the world,*
> *the unreasonable one persists in trying to adapt the world to himself.*
> *Therefore, all progress depends on the unreasonable man. From memory,*
> *it was probably in the early 1980s, I remember reading that and*
> *thinking, 'Wow!' That opened my mind. I've used this joke about being*
> *unreasonable and people have called me unreasonable. And I think that's*

a positive because I love change. If change is necessary, and if you have to be unreasonable to achieve change well, then by all means be unreasonable and be proud. I think that's what inspired me.

For all the bravery, vision, strength and compassion shown by the leaders interviewed, it was interesting to find that a consistent, overtly negative reaction occurred when they were called 'heroes'. That was not what they were wanting, there was no agenda. That was not the point, according to Rani Raad of CNN:

I don't know if I hide it under the cape or if I just don't know when others see it or when you see it, but for me, it's more instinctive. I didn't read a lot of books about this. I didn't read a lot of books about dealing with this. I didn't read a lot. I didn't go researching ways of dealing with trauma and crises. There was none of that. I think for me, I'm kind of lucky, I say lucky because the feedback I get has always been relatively positive, but I'm able to dig into my toolkit of sorts and go beyond empathy and get to what I would call more compassion because I think part and parcel of being a good leader is you have to start with empathy. If you don't have that, then it's a bit of a non-starter for me.

Puneet Chhatwal of IHCL also thought leadership behaviour was inbuilt:

Honestly, it was very intuitive, there is no logic. There are no signs that you should be doing that. And either you are like that or you are not like that. So, either you sit back and wait for things to become OK, and then you very cautiously move ahead. Or by nature, if you take actions as a leader, you have to act and show leadership, whether it comes with risk or without risk, it just happens. So, I would not say that there was some mentoring, counselling, previous reference point, nothing like that. Maybe bad times define who you are.

Through the interviews leaders gave a voice to some of their innermost thoughts. Personally speaking, this was one of the meaningful aspects of this book-creation process. These leaders, these colleagues, all knew in their hearts that when they stood forward, they stood alone. Loneliness was going to be a state of being that they had to accept if they were going to protect the people who were counting on them to take care of them, and take care of what mattered to them. And they were OK with that because the call to leadership was strong enough to move them forward, alone.

CHAPTER 12

NOT IN MY JOB DESCRIPTION: DECIDING TO LEAVE, NOT LEAD

I understand that people who even in the medical world said, 'You know what, I'm not stepping up. I'm worried that I could actually harm somebody that I love.' I understand that, and I think that adds another layer in terms of who stepped up and who didn't.

DR SANJAY GUPTA, CNN CHIEF MEDICAL CORRESPONDENT

Up to this point, the focus of this book has been on those who have stepped up when they heard a calling. They took a decision to actively accept risk, to embrace fear, to master their emotions, and to help others find safety. We have studied them. We have sought to understand their thought processes, their priorities, their patterns of behaviour. We have heard them speak of their silent pains in leading, accepting these as part their duty, part of what it means, and takes, to be a leader. We have accepted their desire to stay out of the limelight, focusing on the tasks ahead of them and those around them.

Interestingly, we have also discovered that when their calling was heard and their wiring was fully activated it caused these people to feel so alive! These leaders felt that they had tapped into the essence of who they are as humans. The act of leading in moments of challenge fulfilled their purpose even if that purpose was never formally articulated, that responsibility was never formally in print, and the outcome was unknown. They found that it was worth the risk because the reward, the feeling of connection, the ability to help others, was their driving force. On hearing their calling, they were unable to do anything but step forward to take leadership, taking care of those who looked to them and trusted them for safety, be it personally or professionally. And after the crisis, they felt a distinct sense of strength, peace and fulfilment.

The human desire to take care of one another is something that Dr Gupta, CNN's Chief Medical Correspondent, feels is very much in our wiring. He is a firm believer in the concept of reciprocal altruism, recognising that we feel good when we take care of one another. As Dr Gupta says:

It actually feels good to do good. It feels good to take care of somebody else, to conduct acts of charity, to help somebody, whatever it might be. The idea that you get so much satisfaction from doing the work compensates for the other things. I think that would be the case during COVID as well. And in some ways, you are better about taking care of yourself when you're getting tremendous joy and satisfaction out of your work.

His belief is that we are born this way, that this innate desire to help others, family, friends, colleagues, community members, is in our wiring from the start. Which begs the question: if something happens in our life that fuses our wiring, that drives us to step forward into a position of leadership, what about those who chose to step aside, leaving instead of leading? What were the thought processes in their minds, the wiring that they possessed, that enabled them to say 'no, this is not my responsibility, this is not where my focus needs to be, this is not my risk to take'.

It would be remiss to not explore this important aspect of decision-making in crisis and how it impacts on leadership. Why? Because the decision to lead versus leave is not black and white. There is a spectrum of colours, a range of considerations, that needs to be understood. Otherwise, it is simply too easy to judge and be disrespectful of the circumstances of others. Also, it would not enhance our ability to help others, both during a crisis and after.

WIRED TO LEAVE

During the crisis, especially in the early days, reactions were very raw, real and rapid. Wiring kicked in. Many leaders around us suddenly started to step up. They attracted our attention. They offered us confidence and calm. They kept our eyes focused forward, even if the view ahead was growing increasingly dark. Many of these leaders are profiled in this book.

But then there were others, those who seemed to step out. We no longer saw them online, on virtual stages, on conference calls, in webinars. We heard from them less and less. We lost contact even socially. Sadly, for many people these leaders caused confusion. For some they even provoked anger, leaving people questioning: 'How could they just leave? They were here to lead! How could they leave me alone?'

These reactions were natural. If we think back to the early days of a crisis we have faced in our lives, no doubt we have all felt emotions of this type about someone, somewhere, at some point. As stated many times in this book, a crisis has the power to leave people feeling painfully alone. At the same time, when a crisis occurs, everyone impacted reacts in different ways, making different choices for different reasons. This is especially true in the early stages of a crisis when physical and emotional panic and pandemonium can reduce our ability to think about anything but ourselves. The more we understand about the wiring of those who made a decision to leave, the more we can:

- help ourselves work through our own reactions to their actions
- liberate ourselves from any feeling of personal rejection or abandonment
- focus our attention and energies on other forms of support
- learn what support they needed to face their own challenges
- protect our ability to maintain a relationship with them once the storm has passed

UNDERSTANDING THE UNDERLYING REASONS

So, why would someone choose to *not* be there for us when we needed them? When those who we know reveal aspects of themselves that are new to us and feel strangely out of character, untrusting or disloyal, our sense of aloneness grows. Instinctively we whisper, 'Where were you when I needed you?'

Again, the reaction – your reaction – is natural. It is not, however, without blind spots. There are reasons others react in the way they do and we need to understand them.

Just as some had a time in their lives when they felt they were called to lead, others had a moment where they felt they needed to leave. Also, there are many ways in which a person can leave. And these reasons may be far more considered, far more serious, than we even remotely comprehend. Again, the situation is not black and white.

Let's first look closely at what it means to leave. The act of leaving can occur in a number of ways. Yes, it may be stepping away completely, separating oneself from those choosing to lead, and even those choosing to follow the leader. Leaving can also be the act of stepping aside to support someone else who is deemed to be the right person to lead at that time, under those circumstances. It may be someone deemed more qualified, courageous, or best suited in terms of character and chemistry to lead in that moment of crisis. A person may feel they are simply unable to lead in one aspect of their lives, i.e. at work, when others need them to take the lead somewhere else, i.e. at home.

> *What is important to remember is that not leading does not mean not caring.*

So, why would someone choose to leave in any of these contexts? What was the hard conversation that these individuals had to have with themselves? There are so many possible reasons, so many colours on the spectrum between black and white.

The choice to leave may occur for a number of personal or professional reasons. Some people leave their roles in a crisis to protect themselves. They were wired to think of self-protection first. As with those wired to lead, the wiring of those who choose to leave may have been set at different times in their life. It may have been when they were children, a time when they chose flight to remove themselves from danger. It may have been a moment when the danger they faced was physical: a house fire, a bully in the playground, a shooter in a mall. Or it may have been emotional, such as a parental argument or an emotionally abusive coach. Something encouraged them to immediately seek shelter rather than to face risk. Or their moment of wiring may have happened as adults, when they chose the option of flight to separate themselves in a competition or as a way of protecting themselves in conflict.

Whatever the circumstances, whatever the crisis, some people are wired to protect themselves first. Again, this does not mean they chose to leave others in a position of risk. Their lens was simply set on zoom, the wider-angle perspective was not visible.

There are also, however, those who chose to leave because their wide-angle lens was acutely focused on others who they knew also needed them. It may have been family, close friends, neighbours, community leaders, or many others. The option of leaving one situation and set of people was necessary to protect others, not to protect themselves.

This choice faced many leaders we thought would have stepped forward. They were simply unable to stay because they had to keep others out of harm's way. Someone, something, somewhere else was their priority. In the opening quote of this chapter, Dr Gupta referred to medical practitioners, who are wired to respond to those in need. They are the first to step up. This commitment to stepping up is at the heart of their profession and of their vocation. But some medical practitioners knew that by engaging with people suffering from COVID-19, they were going to put loved ones at high risk. They were unable to take that risk because those around them were unable to endure the damage that might have been caused by COVID-19, particularly if they had other underlying medical conditions. These leaders chose to step out; they did it for others. The calling they heard was stronger elsewhere.

How can we ever know what is happening in others' homes? In their hearts? How can we possibly feel the challenge of their decision-making?

I reminded my team that we must never presume to understand what is happening behind other people's computer screens. Just as we can never truly know what is happening behind the closed doors, devices and connections of others, so too can they never know what is happening behind ours.

FACING THE 'AFTER'

In all cases, whether someone chose to step up or step out, they had to make a decision, and they had to live with it. And it can be extremely difficult to live with a decision made in a moment of crisis. Those who are wired to lead, often decided to accept any risk knowing that they could not look themselves in the mirror if they didn't step forward to help.

For those who have been wired to leave a known place and group of people, being able to look oneself in the mirror after the crisis has passed can be a greater challenge. These individuals may face an 'after' that can bring with it a myriad of emotions which may turn into significant psychological burdens. They may face a feeling of guilt, a painful sense of abandoning others who trusted them for direction and protection. They may face anger, loathing themselves for having failed as a family member, as a leader, as a colleague, as a friend. They may face embarrassment and feel deeply uncomfortable facing those they left behind, knowing and understanding their disappointment. They may face regret, cursing themselves for not having done what now, with time and clarity, they know they should have. Or they may face isolation, literally or figuratively feeling cut off, left behind, the world having moved on without them.

As we never really know what others are going through, their pressures, their priorities, their suffering, their sadness, their self-negotiation, we should not underestimate their burden in the 'after'.

> *In the aftermath of a crisis, compassion must be shown to all who have suffered and endured the crisis, whatever their decision may have been. All those who chose to leave must be reconnected with the community and embraced as much as those who chose to lead. This is a vital part of 'building a better after'.*

Leaders must work to enable others to understand why decisions were made, why some chose to lead and others chose to leave. It is important that leaders help people to rebuild trust, rebuild connections and rebuild shared purpose with all those returning to the industry, wherever they may be within the ecosystem. Leaders need to inspire others to support one another so that all involved and affected are able to pull through, together, whatever their decision was in their moment.

How can this be done? This is where, not just during but also in the aftermath of a crisis, leaders need to connect with the humanity of others, and themselves. Reflecting on a crisis we have experienced in our lives we have all seen actions taken, heard comments made, seen messages sent, and witnessed outbreaks of emotion that have surprised us, and not in a good way. These were not just things done by others, they are things we also did in the heat of the moment, in exceptionally challenging times of crisis. By encouraging forgiveness, the scars can be healed, the bonds can be rebuilt, the future can be without a long shadow to the past.

There can be no judgement. There must only be compassion with others, and compassion with oneself, for as expressed by the WHO, a crisis is not over anywhere until it is over everywhere.

CHAPTER 13

A WHISPER TO MOTHER NATURE: EXPRESSING GRATITUDE EVEN IN THE HARDEST OF TIMES

Thank you that it wasn't worse.

GEOFFREY KENT, FOUNDER AND OWNER OF ABERCROMBIE & KENT (A&K)

Whichever way we look at it, however we reflect upon the pandemic, whatever good or bad we are able to make of it and take from it, echoing what was said right at the beginning of this book, the fact is this: it was hard.

And for millions upon millions, it still is.

The crisis hit all of us. Differently, yes, but it hit all of us, all at once. For a period of time, for the first time in our lives, everyone, everywhere was forced to live alone, work alone, learn alone, laugh alone, cry alone and especially grieve alone. And for many, it forced them to die alone.

Such is the case with any crisis that stops, rocks and reshapes our lives, whether personal or professional, local or global, recent past or after a significant passage of time. It can be incredibly hard to find a beam of sunlight through the darkness. And so sometimes you just need to reach for a flashlight, some source of brightness, no matter how small, to help us make sense of it all and take something good from it.

The Call to Leadership has given leaders a platform to share their personal stories and insights, giving us a unique understanding of how they approach challenges and crises. They have revealed how they are wired, how they found strength to endure and inspire others during challenging times, how they understand their own ability to respond to crisis, and how they were able to maintain faith in the future. Through their experiences and our own, we have seen and felt the deeply personal changes that have occurred in a multitude of aspects of our daily lives. Most notably, we have seen changes in the many values of health, nutrition, space, movement, communication, technology, travel, nature, community, small businesses, essential workers and our connection to ourselves.

And yet now, as you are reading this, that time can feel like a lifetime ago. Masks are off, mobility restrictions are removed. The world is back to business, shaking hands, taking a seat at the boardroom table, gathering in conference halls, on the aircraft, wherever people are being asked to 'show up'. Forgetting is all too easy and few signs of those challenging times remain. We see no milestone markers, masks or memories people choose to hold onto. Why remember? Why hold on to those times, looking back when we need to move forward, rapidly, with no regrets?

Fast-forwarding without an understanding of, and respect for, the past would waste, even insult, the call to action we all heard, and felt, to different degrees. The understanding we take away from the pandemic goes beyond what businesses, governments, academics and others are reported to have experienced and analysed. It goes beyond the well-packaged, widely profiled and promoted analyses that are often used to predict the future by those in high positions of power, such as the C-suites and state authorities. It goes farther, and it goes deeper.

SEEING THE LIGHT THROUGH THE DARKNESS

Having endured a crisis, our personal, often unspoken, internal understanding is also critical. It helps us find meaning and it initiates healing. Central to this is our need to understand simply, *why*?

Why did this happen?

Why me?

Why us?

Why now?

This goes beyond the *what* and the *how*. It is so much deeper and more personal than questioning:

- What exactly has happened?
- What am I supposed to learn from it?
- What am I supposed to gain from it?
- How do I get past the devastation of it?
- How do I get past the anger?
- How do I find peace?

The ability to find meaning is one of the ways of finding, in the immediate term, a sense of control. In the intermediate term, a sense of peace. And in the longer term, healing. Linked to this is finding accountability – someone to blame and somewhere to channel all the raw emotion that pours out as reality sinks in. Who had the greatest level of connection to all that happened to cause the crisis? Who had the greatest influence and, even for a moment, control, over all that went so out of control?

Establishing some sense of clarity can help one break free from being stuck in the moment. It lessens the intensity of darkness faced, allowing a sliver of light to break through. As made clear throughout this book, blame is cast in one singular direction: Mother Nature. Who else could have unleashed a force so improbable to occur, impossible to understand, unstoppable in scale and speed, and undeniable in intent? And who else could we all look to for some sense of reason that would not unleash active rage? Only Mother Nature had the ability to ground us all, to stop us all, to force us to think, to gain perspective, and to prioritise. And, as we saw as a global community, for the first time in our generation, she forced us to come together as one united force, bonded by a humanitarian spirit that wanted to see others, those we loved, and even those we didn't know, simply survive. Mother Nature was defining the strength, the ferocity, and the grace of this entire time.

Mother Nature is to be blamed. Equally, one can argue that Mother Nature is to be credited. Mother Nature gave us a chance to take care of ourselves, and those we care for. Framing the crisis as an act of Mother Nature provided a way of finding some sort of reason behind all the devastation, a target for anger – a natural response to an unnatural crisis.

There must be a way of channelling all the upset. There must be a way of pushing past all the destruction and the damage to life, to heal the scars. For this reason, this book carefully examined how leaders responded to Mother Nature as the cause of this crisis. This enabled me to understand not just their relationship with Mother Nature, a force at the heart of these challenging times, but how, after all the damage caused, they would find meaning to enable them to take the first steps forward in helping and healing.

In the interviews, a straightforward question was posed to all of our leaders:

IF YOU WERE TO WHISPER 'THANK YOU' TO MOTHER NATURE, WHAT WOULD YOU THANK HER FOR?

Almost all the leaders thanked her for forcing us to look closely at what mattered.

What mattered in the lives that we have.

Who mattered.

And *why* we mattered.

They each knew without a moment of hesitation, and without a filter on their words or emotions, that for which they would give thanks. For some it was about the gift of connection. Brad Dean of Discover Puerto Rico said:

> *Thank you for the pause, the pause on relentless activity that distracts us and consumes us at the same time. Thank you for the reminders of the gifts that we've been entrusted with but need protection – people and the environment. Thank you for the connectivity. As much as we were all at home sequestered, there was a human bond that was there to be nourished. Now it took some technology to make that happen, but in a weird way, as much as we were all separated, we were more connected. And I guess that's part of just coming through a crisis together. But I think Mother Nature delivered that and on a very practical level.*

Matthew Upchurch of Virtuoso commented:

> *I would say thank you for reminding us how precious life is and how everything is interconnected. And I think that the vast majority of human suffering comes when we are somehow out of fear or fear based. We somehow think that we're not connected. That we're separate.*

Fred Dixon of NYC Tourism + Conventions answered:

> *I would thank her for the gift of life. I think from the very beginning, this was not about a government conspiracy theory, that this was not 'What's behind this?' To me, I knew this was Mother Nature. This absolutely was. I never questioned in my heart that this was part of evolution, that this was part of God's plan in one way or another. There is great solace in that, in the sense that this is the way Mother Nature operates. We have to recognise that we coexist in this world. This is not our planet entirely*

in that way. And so, the humbling reminder that life is about balance is a lasting one for me. I think thanking her for the gift of life in this sense is probably what I would do.

Gavin Tollman of TTC reflected:

If we can make the right decisions, as humanity does, we must make the right decisions. I don't think it's too late. I think we can reverse some of the short-sighted decisions of mankind and I was enamoured by how quickly Mother Nature took back city centres. How nature was able to restore itself so quickly. And so, it does give me optimism that, even though we appear to be on the wrong trajectory, leadership can actually do the right thing and we can reverse the tide. We have an opportunity for reinvention, and the reinvention permeates everything we do. One of the things I'm enjoying most at the moment is how we can work; hybrid working models, greater engagement with our staff. Looking at how we can genuinely make travel matter in a new world. Not in theory but doing it with such a degree of intent.

Kimarli Fernando of Sri Lanka's tourism board said:

I would thank her for making people realise the value of nature, value of people, value of eating vegetarian, eating healthy, value of vegetation, value of yoga. I'm a strong Buddhist. So, for me, that guided me a lot. I believe in Buddhism. It says that the world will not get destroyed. We will destroy the world. People will destroy with the same sense that they did many centuries ago. So, he said, people will destroy this, but the world will be there. We will keep destroying it. And we will be born again and wherever in heaven or hell or on this earth. But I feel through COVID, I have seen so many of my friends, my family, people, have changed for the better.

Puneet Chhatwal of IHCL saw positive change:

It was a true test for myself, my team, the values we stood for, it all came out together and just set us apart from everybody else. You know 'A Psalm of Life' by Longfellow: 'Lives of great men all remind us, we can make our lives sublime, and departing, leave behind us, footprints on the sands of time.' So, I think the footprints on the sands of time that we have left is not only a difficult act for others to follow, but a difficult act for us. Because we had started the journey with Aspiration 2022, COVID

accelerated that journey and opened up the hearts and minds of more
people who might have been passively resisting the change. They also were
open to that change. And the change was not to completely change who
you are. The change was to keep everything that is great from the past but
complement it with some of the newer things happening around us,
or which will take us forward for the next five, ten, fifteen, twenty years.

Some leaders were thankful that Mother Nature made them responsible for
taking care of others, and for taking care of themselves. Fahd Hamidaddin
of STA shared these sentiments:

Thank you for the wakeup call. Thank you for making us take stock of
one another. Thank you for giving us a moment of reflection to make the
best choices of what baggage to carry forward and what to leave behind.

Hon. Najib Balala said:

We never appreciated life. We never appreciated family. We never
appreciated the privileges we have in waking up and working, coordinating
and even travelling. These are the things we have taken for granted.

Other leaders focused on global issues that the global community needed
to see as a priority, as Julia Simpson of the WTTC explained:

I wouldn't whisper 'thank you'. I think I'd shout 'thank you' because I
think it's our biggest challenge. Climate change, sustainability, protecting
and loving nature, absolutely centre stage.

Professor Demian Hodari of EHL noticed:

We are really not as powerful as we think. Unfortunately, it came through
a lot of death and mayhem, but I think it is always reminding people that
we need to be more respectful of the earth. I just feel like we forgot already,
we're forgetting. People forget about the pandemic and people forget about
climate issues. And we are already more worried about how we are going
to get gas for our cars for the next six months or heat our homes rather than
the pandemic and climate change. And now this should really be helping
us to find different solutions. So, thank you for giving us that reminder, but
come on, you need to remind us more powerfully.

Marloes Knippenberg of Kerten Hospitality said:

> *I thank you for giving us such a strong message of realisation, and kind of going: 'Guys, you are going to do something, or not. It's your choice. But let me show you something …'*

Some leaders were simply thankful for Mother Nature's mercy, including Rani Raad of CNN:

> *Thank you for letting us off that easy.*

There were of course those leaders who absolutely would *not* express thanks to Mother Nature and thought her 'lessons' came at too high a cost, such as Willie Walsh of IATA:

> *No, I'm sorry. I wouldn't. Mother Nature is a bitch. This was tough. I think she could have slapped us a little bit more gently. This has been a horrible period for everybody. I think you do go through a period like this, and you appreciate things more, the things you took for granted. You do appreciate it. I think of what some people had to go through in lockdown where they couldn't go out, they couldn't play sports which, to me, I couldn't understand that, but you couldn't go out and do the things that we all encourage people to do, get out there and play some football, exercise, eat healthily.*

The personal learnings we take from a crisis, the inner voice we hear in both our hearts and our heads as a deeply moving whisper that somehow provides us with some sense of meaning, do not present themselves as obviously, nor audibly. And yet they are there to be witnessed quietly and subtly, sometimes in individuals standing right beside us. And importantly, in ourselves.

CHAPTER 14

REFLECTIONS: LIVING THE LEADERSHIP LEARNINGS

There's a difference between confidence and cockiness or arrogance. It's that quiet sort of knowledge that you have inside that you're up to the task, whatever it is that is going to be confronting you.

DAN RICHARDS, CEO, GLOBAL RESCUE

There is so much that leaders have shared through their lives and their learnings to help me to create one single narrative. There are too many moments, too many memories, too many lessons. But the fact remains that this book, this calling, would not have honoured *you* as a reader if it did not provide you with very real reasons to have confidence in your ability to face challenges and find your way to the eye of the storm and then out to a better after. Your time investment as a reader is significant. It is time you are investing in listening to the voices of others, hearing the lessons of others, sharing times in their lives, and giving up time in your life.

So, what has this time given us? The hope is that this book has provided ways of strengthening our ability to face whatever is ahead and come through stronger. For all of the uncertainty that the future holds there is one thing we can be certain of, we will at some point in our lives face the next crisis, and then the next, and then the next. What these crises may turn out to be we cannot know. It may be an incident of scale, an extreme weather event, another pandemic, a mass attack, that galvanises us to come together as one community, or it may be a personal loss of a loved one or a professional loss of a job that makes us feel so very alone. Regardless of the specifics and the circumstances, the feeling of loss is a common thread, whether it is loss of stability, security, faith or focus.

> *Somehow, a breakthrough happens that enables some leaders to find a solid, secure, quiet place not simply in their world, but in themselves. It is a confidence that calms their thoughts and resulting actions and creates a sense of calm in others.*

Through the development of this book, leaders were open and honest in sharing their own understanding, and their own learnings, around:

How they were able to hush the noise to be able to hear their calling.

How they were able to find the strength to step forward. Where. And even from whom.

How they were able to keep things in perspective.

Leaders who hear their calling and take action demonstrate distinct characteristics, capabilities and courage, as well as compassion. They possess an innate understanding of how to access and mobilise their strength with certainty and also humility. By following their example and understanding, we can learn how to take on challenges that we too will undoubtedly face and unlock our own ability to fight.

So, what have we discovered so far? How can we break through fear and gain even a tiny sense of control, and therefore calm? Let's take a closer look at what our leaders shared about their ability to find their way to the eye of the storm and safely through to the other side, sometimes even stronger.

1. READING THE RISK

First and foremost, it is vitally important to read the risk and immediately assess, subconsciously and instinctively, the presence of a threat. How? Ask the following questions to assess the situation, and its impact:

- What exactly is happening?
  - What is the danger being faced?
  - What is the source?
  - What is the severity?

- Is it a direct threat?
  - To me physically and/or emotionally?
  - To others for whom I am responsible?
  - What impact can it have on me?
  - What impact can it have on others?
  - To the world in which I/we live?
  - To the world in which I/we operate?

- Is it an indirect threat?
  - Around us physically and/or emotionally?

- Around others for whom we are responsible?
- How can it impact me and/or others?
- How can it impact our direct world?
- How can it impact our wider world?

Having assessed the risk, identify areas where one can take control as a leader. Without hesitation, leaders believed that it was important to define areas of potential control as soon as possible. With emotions running high, finances running low, and people's imaginations running in every direction of doom, focusing on what you cannot control cannot help you. And it certainly cannot calm you.

> *Being crystal clear on what is within one's*
> *control is critical to taking control.*

2. DEFINING THE POSSIBLE DAMAGE

Having read the risk, the next step is accepting that there may very well be severe loss of revenue, jobs, investments and livelihoods. There may even be heart-breaking losses of lives, relationships and futures. Leaders explained that while there is a very real risk of losses, one can find strength by controlling the scale of the loss. This can be done in a number of ways:

1. Establishing the worst-case scenario, including the impact on jobs and revenues.
2. Clarifying the metrics that matter to weather the storm, such as minimising profit and job losses, minimising furlough programmes, redeploying people, upskilling and educating to support people and finding new opportunities inside and outside of the business.
3. Communicating to others the elements of risk and opportunity for control, including managing and measuring the risks, identifying the priorities and actions to manage direct risks, and determining if the situation is permanent to help your team stay focused, calm, confident, transparent and united.

Putting the risk into context, looking the scary numbers directly in the eye, and feeling some sense of control over their own fears of 'what if?' enables leaders to find a way of taming the fire and activates their own sense of inner calm.

3. BEING INSPIRED BY ONE'S 'WHY'

Understanding one's sense of duty, what motivates that sense of duty, is sometimes termed one's 'why'. The fact that one is trusted by others to step forward and take care of others is a very powerful motivator. It might come from:

- heads of state or other government officials looking to their leaders within cabinet to safeguard their country
- royal families looking to their people and leaders to take care of the nation and protect citizens and themselves
- boards of directors needing leaders to protect their profits, their people and their brand
- deans and other academic staff needing leaders to ensure their students receive a good education
- families, needing their loved ones to simply keep them safe

> *Everyone needs to have someone or something to fight for. Recognising and embracing that motivation, that calling, is profoundly powerful. It becomes a part of one's identity and pride. It inspires clarity, strength and greatness within us that we often didn't realise we had.*

4. LEADERSHIP PRESENCE IS ESSENTIAL

For those stepping up to lead, the ability to stay centred and confident is innate. For others, however, a crisis can leave them feeling abandoned, unvalued, and even unworthy if they are left to feel alone. For this reason, the ongoing presence of a leader is a non-negotiable. Presence can be felt through various formats, each with their own invaluable ability to convey various messages through various messengers.

WORDS MATTER

As explained, for those facing a crisis establishing a sense of control is vital. This applies to both leaders and followers. We all in our respective places, spaces and spheres of influence need to rapidly get a sense of what is happening, why, where, to whom, and the aspects we always want to get a grasp on, for how long.

The language of leaders has a central part to play in this quest for control. Clarity, transparency and honesty are non-negotiables. Through the humanity of communication exercised by leaders, followers are able to easily accept and adopt the information they recognise as critical. Also, they appreciate the changes required in understanding and guidance as a crisis unfolds and evolves.

Leaders must communicate with conviction to be accepted with credibility and confidence by followers.

OPTICS MATTER

The language of leaders comes through not only what they say, but how they appear. Body language plays a huge role in reinforcing a message. It goes a long way in building connection, expressing compassion, demonstrating confidence and establishing credibility. Poor body language can and does create suspicion, distrust, disconnects. Posture matters, eye contact matters, hand gestures matter. Settings matter, styling matters, symbols matter.

MOMENTUM MATTERS

When a situation generates fear and anxiety, when confusion abounds, it is important that leaders ensure they maintain strong lines of communication. In so doing they will be able to embed:

- clarity of the freshest possible information
- alignment of required action
- monitoring and management of individual well-being
- connection across the follower community
- sustained focus on a successful 'after'

As stated earlier, leaders need to navigate others through their individual *fight, flight* or *freeze* responses. If this is not managed, it can make a crisis situation worse.

5. BUILDING THAT BETTER 'AFTER'

Finally, it is important to always keep an eye on the 'after'. No one leaves a crisis unaffected, unchanged, unwounded. The scars may not be visible, but they are there. They may be physical, they may be emotional. Whatever the case, they are there.

One of the hardest parts of leadership during a crisis is not only helping people find their way to the eye of the storm, but faith that they will get through it and may, just may, find a rainbow on the other side. This requires helping those around them to:

- establish a sense of stability
- feel a sense of unity
- identify possible areas of opportunity
- unlock a spirit of creativity
- imagine a stronger 'after' as a very real, exciting possibility
- stay focused on working to make it a reality

Critically and as examined earlier, building that 'after' applies to both those who chose to stay and lead, and those who chose to leave during the crisis. As hard as it may be, leaders need to find the strength and compassion to help others rebuild trust, respect and connections. No one must ever be left to stand alone during, or after, a crisis.

CHAPTER 15

TWENTY LEADERS HONOURED: THE PEOPLE BEHIND THE LEADERSHIP PERSONALITIES

*I learned that courage was not the absence of fear,
but the triumph over it. The brave man is not he who
does not feel afraid, but he who conquers that fear.*

SOUTH AFRICAN PRESIDENT, NELSON MANDELA

The Call to Leadership received the immense complement of an unusually high level of acceptance of requests to be interviewed for the book, by an exceptionally high level of global leadership across the travel and tourism space. Yes, these were people known to me personally through professional contact. They were not, however, people obliged to support this project.

And yet they gave me their time.

They gave of their insight and intelligence.

And importantly, richly, humbly, beautifully, and often surprisingly to themselves, they gave of themselves.

TWENTY REMARKABLE INTERVIEWS, THREE RICH LAYERS OF DISCOVERY

On the surface, we discovered that which was *interesting*. The interesting decisions that leaders made, processes that they went through, techniques of placing things in context. This was interesting to me as creator of this book, and importantly, interesting to my interviewees who had never before thought about their own ability to hear their calling, to step forward, to courageously lead. These elements are called out in this book because they are levers that can be used as resources in the future to help us assess exactly what is happening when we feel a crisis unfolding, and how to respond and find our way in the eye of the storm.

On top of the interesting, there were the *insightful* moments of revelation that came through. Leaders exposed a depth of understanding that many can often completely overlook. The insight that was provided gave richness to the resources of intelligence that came through. Insight was also shown in how the leaders were processing what was happening, and crucially, how they helped carry not just others through the crisis but themselves.

And then there was the *intimate* sharing that came through the interviews, which could be tear-provoking. It is this intimacy of sharing that has added a layer of understanding to the quest of *The Call to Leadership*, to understand the wiring of leaders and how they behave during crisis. In addition, this intimacy revealed the true humanity behind these leaders, their compassion, their vulnerability, their sensitivity. These attributes ultimately turned them into some of the most admired leaders that we have around us in our world. This intimacy of sharing often took them by surprise, and it remains in my mind and heart, as the author of this book. It uniquely separates what these leaders have shared in the hundreds of interviews they had already given during the pandemic, and what they shared when they came for their one-on-one interview for *The Call to Leadership*.

Importantly, they shared what they had never articulated before in their own minds. They were grateful to realise that what makes them good leaders goes far beyond their technical expertise. It is about their compassion. It is about their humanity, it is about their heart, and it is about their courage. All of these elements combined helped them to get through this last crisis. They also reflect a fundamental belief that through all these challenges, we can indeed come through better people, not just better leaders.

Each of the leaders participating in this book has shared their experience of not only the global crisis of COVID-19, but also the crises they endured as far back as when they were young children. Their rich, insightful, in-depth revelation of their own experiences was to a level beyond anything ever anticipated. These leaders opened themselves up to this project in a way that has elevated insight, analysis and my writing. They showed that they too were human, something often recognised by onlookers when leaders seemingly fearlessly step forward into the flames.

They too feel fear.

They too suffer loss.

They too question '*Why?*'

They too fall ill from the virus.

And importantly, they look for leadership.

SEEKING PERSONAL CLOSURE

Why did these leaders agree to participate in this project and reflect on a time that many wish to forget? Each of the leaders participating in this project was asked exactly this:

WHY DID YOU SAY 'YES'?

Clearly there was a greater 'why' that they held in their hearts that needed a response. They let me in close, they let me get remarkably close, moving from what was interesting and what was insightful to what was deeply intimate.

They did it for, I believe, several reasons, including a desire within them to dig deeper, as expressed by Paul Griffiths of DAA:

> *Immediately I thought this isn't going to be a Bloomberg interview where they're going to push me on government funding, subsidies and all those really boring things. I think something we share is that we are propelled by the emotional energy that sits within us. Right. Would you agree with that? And I find that's a driving force and I feel very motivated when I find kindred spirits that are also motivated by that. So of course, I said yes straight away.*

> *It became very clear that the interviewees were not talking to the interviewer. They were sharing with themselves.*

Brad Dean of Discover Puerto Rico said:

> *It would be really heartbreaking if we as an industry don't come out of this with important lessons learned that are carried forward. And admittedly so many of us, I put myself on this list, have done exactly what you just mentioned. We've rushed right back into how we get the engine moving again and how do we grow travel and tourism? But a few key leaders, yourself especially, are taking time to put everything in perspective, that is really the hope that will carry forward and educate and inform us. So, to me, if I can contribute anything of value, that's going to help someone be better prepared to lead through this in the future.*

Fred Dixon of NYC Tourism + Conventions replied:

> *I think you are a student of history in the same way I am, in the sense that we have to record these moments and, in a way, we have to preserve them. We have to learn from them. I'm a big believer in that. I've been in NYC & Company now for seventeen years and we have shared the 9/11 case study with countless destinations and people around the world.*
>
> *People want to know how we recovered from 9/11, what happened in the days immediately after what happened, in the years after, and what's the legacy. It's very natural for us to document and to share experiences, for the better of all, because we all are being tested right now in small and big ways. When I knew that you were documenting this and you were going to be talking to people that were in the eye of the storm, I knew that it would be important for New York's perspective to be part of that. I was honoured that you asked me, and I think this is going to be a tremendous resource for people.*

Matthew Upchurch of Virtuoso:

> *If you had the privilege, the honour and the opportunity to lead and make a positive difference, then you need to say 'yes'. When you described what you were doing, if I could add anything that is of help and is useful to anybody, I was going to say 'yes'. To know that when you get up every day, that something that you and your team did has made a positive difference in somebody else's life is one of humanity's greatest gifts.*

Darrell Wade of Intrepid said:

> *It might be a bit of a platform for change. I just think any opportunity to talk about how we can change society and take a more values-based approach to society, then that's good. If someone reads about things like that, then they start to learn, and they start to hopefully open their mind a little bit as to how we can effect change for the future.*

Hon. Najib Balala said:

> *I know we have a responsibility as leaders, not only in this sector, but global leaders, to say, 'What can we do to show the world we can be better?' And that's why I said yes. We have done, I've done my part. Maybe somebody else can do it better. But when you asked me to do this,*

automatically I said yes. This is important. We need to have case studies, not only of leaders, how they lead, but on crises like this, because we never learn our lessons. And today, if we put everything into perspective, I've told my office to do that as well. So, the next leader who comes in will have it ready so that it will be easier to improve, and easier to react or to act when crisis comes.

Kimarli Fernando of Sri Lanka's tourism board:

I want to see what others have said, and I want to learn. I think that everybody keeps learning. I think what Sri Lanka has is special. I wanted people to know what Sri Lanka did. I have pride in my country and respect for the people I worked with. I would like to show them that I got the chance and I spoke, in respect for them actually. Yeah, to show my country.

Gavin Tollman of TTC said:

We have an opportunity for reinvention, and the reinvention permeates everything we do. One of the things I'm enjoying most at the moment is how we can actually genuinely make travel matter in a new world, not in theory, but doing it with such a degree of intent.

Puneet Chhatwal of IHCL stated:

It is a part of building relationships, meaningful relationships, where it's not just about you shining, it's all of us collectively doing things which matter. And we may or may not agree with one of the decisions. But the majority have a bond amongst like-minded people. And then it overlaps and overlaps and overlaps. And it's very infectious. It's stronger than COVID-19 I would say.

Furthermore, there was an underlying need to have a final word. The discussions revealed a common desire for closure, even if it was subconscious, among all those who took part. The leaders wanted to look back at this time and find something positive, something to be grateful for and able to appreciate what happened, not only curse it. Crucially, they also wished to survey the landscape ahead and decide how they came through this time stronger not just as a person but professionally, and not just as someone in the travel and tourism industry, but someone within the global community.

For these leaders, this was a humanitarian challenge within the context of an industry. They recognised that it is a humanitarian challenge that brought the best of humanity and themselves to the fore. They wanted to contribute this perspective to the book.

Finally, they knew that ultimately this was going to be a project which would subtly and with deep sincerity say thank you for everything they have done. These leaders have never sought fame or praise. Still, they are all human. And sometimes they, like all of us, just need to hear a genuine, gentle and loving whisper of 'I see you' and 'I thank you'.

PROFESSIONAL PROFILES

HON. NAJIB BALALA

(FORMER) MINISTER OF TOURISM & WILDLIFE, KENYA

A proud son of Kenya, Najib Balala was reappointed as Cabinet Secretary for Tourism and Wildlife in the Republic of Kenya in 2015, serving in the role until 2022, making him the nation's longest-serving Tourism Minister. During his final tenure he delivered the Tourism Bill and gave the sector a policy and legal framework geared towards maintaining sustainability. He also served the government of Kenya in various other ministerial roles throughout his accomplished career. Najib now serves as Vice-President of Fauna and Flora International (FFI), a top wildlife conservation charity, as well as the Saudi-based Sustainable Tourism Global Centre. Over many years, he has championed wildlife conservation, with a mission to protect the world's wildlife species for future generations. At a global tourism level, the scope and scale of both his local and international expertise and the respect he commanded resulted in his being elected Chairman of the UNWTO Executive Council.

HTTPS://WWW.TOURISM.GO.KE

PUNEET CHHATWAL

MANAGING DIRECTOR & CHIEF EXECUTIVE OFFICER, INDIAN HOTELS COMPANY LIMITED (IHCL)

A global hospitality leader with close to four decades of experience at highly acclaimed hotel groups in Europe and North America, in 2017 Puneet joined the Indian Hotels Company Limited (IHCL) as the Managing Director and CEO. Under Puneet's leadership IHCL has been on a journey of reimagination to achieve not only sustainable profitable growth, but industry-leading innovation in both product and experience development. A champion of organisational culture, he works tirelessly to ensure IHCL's iconic Taj Hotel collection of properties holds 'Tajness' at the heart of service delivery excellence – a mission that has yielded year after year recognition of the Taj brand as #1 in Brand Finance's 'Strongest Indian Brands' report. Prior to joining IHCL he held positions of CEO and member of the executive board of Steigenberger Hotels AG – Deutsche Hospitality and Chief Development Officer of the Rezidor Hotel Group – Carlson Hotels Worldwide.

He also serves as the leading voice of the industry in India through various high-profile, highly trusted positions. Puneet is a graduate of both Delhi University and the Institute of Hotel Management, Delhi. He has an MBA in hospitality from ESSEC, Paris and took an advanced management programme from INSEAD.

HTTPS://WWW.IHCLTATA.COM

BRAD DEAN

CEO, DISCOVER PUERTO RICO

With over twenty years of experience in the travel and tourism industry, Brad Dean assumed the role of CEO for Discover Puerto Rico in July 2018, the island's first destination marketing organisation that supports the promotion of tourism to foster economic growth. Brad began his career in Puerto Rico, working as a financial analyst for General Electric. In 1995, he opened and led the successful Myrtle Beach resort and in 1998, Brad joined the Myrtle Beach Area Chamber of Commerce as its CFO. In 2003, he was named President and CEO of the chamber. Under his leadership the organisation was named Chamber of Commerce of the Year by the American Chamber of Commerce Executives, in 2015. Brad serves in leadership roles in various organisations including the US Travel Association, Destinations International, and Meeting Planners International. He is a member of the National Council State Tourism Directors and also serves on the United States Travel and Tourism Advisory Board.

HTTPS://WWW.DISCOVERPUERTORICO.COM

FRED DIXON

CEO, NEW YORK CITY TOURISM + CONVENTIONS

Serving the travel industry for over thirty years as President and CEO of New York City's official destination marketing organisation, Fred's leadership has been integral to the success of the city's tourism economy. Fred has been with New York City Tourism + Conventions (previously known as NYC & Company) since 2005, previously serving as Vice President before taking on the CEO role in 2014. His responsibilities include developing and implementing strategies that grow global business and leisure travel to NYC through tourism, meetings and events. As a leader in one of America's most popular destinations and populous cities, Fred has led his city's tourism sector through many crises, as he joined NYC & Company just four years after 9/11. In 2020, he used that experience to create the Coalition for NYC Hospitality and Tourism Recovery, an industry-wide initiative that brought together leaders from across the five boroughs of New York City. Supported by a $30 million investment by the City of New York and through the trusted leadership of Fred and his team, the coalition activated a roadmap for tourism recovery. A 'Stay Well NYC' pledge overtly embedded best practice health and safety protocols for visitors and the visited across all tourism stakeholders and their offerings. This project was accompanied by a new revitalisation campaign, 'All In NYC'. Fred also holds leadership positions on boards and committees including the New York Convention Center Operating Corporation Board, the US Travel Association, the Meetings Mean Business Coalition and he is a member of the IPW Planning Committee.

HTTPS://BUSINESS.NYCGO.COM

KIMARLI FERNANDO

(FORMER) HEAD OF SRI LANKA TOURISM, MINISTRY OF TOURISM

A very focused result-oriented individual with over thirty-three years of experience and a proven track record of good corporate governance and ethical practices, Kimarli is a change agent, implementing new strategies and re-engineering organisations. She contributed to a policy framework in 2019 for tourism, tea, pepper, cinnamon, dairy and fisheries. Kimarli is a published author who holds multiple board positions across the financial and corporate sectors after her experience as CEO of Pan Asia Bank.

Kimarli Fernando won Professional Woman of the Year 2007 and Woman of Achievement for Banking 2009. She has always shown determination, commitment and motivation as demonstrated in being the first woman in Sri Lanka to participate in the annual six-mile sea swim, before going on to captain Sri Lanka's national swimming team and competing in the Asian Games. She was also the first female chairperson to head Sri Lanka Tourism, Ministry of Tourism. Kimarli is the secretary for the Sri Lanka Society at the London School of Economics, a member of the human rights society of the Sri Lanka Law College and a life member of the Bar Association of Sri Lanka.

HTTPS://WWW.TOURISMMIN.GOV.LK

PAUL GRIFFITHS

CEO OF DUBAI AIRPORTS

Paul Griffiths is CEO of Dubai Airports, with the responsibility for the operation and development of Dubai International (DXB) – the world's busiest airport for international passengers, as well as Dubai World Central (DWC).

Paul joined Dubai Airports as its first CEO in October 2007. A year later, Paul was instrumental in the flawless launch of Terminal 3 at DXB and in 2010 successfully opened the Emirate's second airport, DWC. He achieved another milestone in Dubai's aviation history on 2 January 2013 with the opening of Concourse A, the world's first purpose-built A380 facility followed by Concourse D in 2016. Paul also oversaw the opening of the passenger terminal at DWC in 2013. On 20 December 2018, Paul joined Dubai Airports' Chairman HH Sheikh Ahmed bin Saeed Al Maktoum in welcoming DXB's billionth passenger.

Under Paul's leadership, Dubai Airports successfully managed the COVID-19 crisis and DXB became one of the first airports to welcome back international tourists. He led the teams at DXB and DWC to support a massive repatriation operation in close coordination with diplomatic missions, UAE authorities, airlines, and other service partners to help nearly half a million people get back to their homes during the first global lockdown in 2020. Paul played a crucial role in the recovery of DXB's operations and growth through travel corridor arrangements with several key markets, as well as by lobbying the industry to push for standardised testing-based travel protocols. Paul spearheaded a campaign to keep the hibernating parts of the airport ready for reopening at very short notice which resulted in the timely and smooth reopening of Terminal 1 and Concourse D in June 2021 and the airport's return to full operational capacity with the reopening of Concourse A in November 2021.

Prior to moving to Dubai, Paul was Managing Director of London's Gatwick Airport. Before joining airport operator BAA in 2004, he spent fourteen years with the Virgin Group, working closely with Sir Richard Branson as a board director of the Virgin Travel Group, responsible for the commercial activities of both Virgin Atlantic Airways and Virgin Trains.

HTTPS://WWW.DUBAIAIRPORTS.AE

FAHD HAMIDADDIN

CEO, SAUDI TOURISM AUTHORITY (STA)

Fahd is the founding CEO of the Saudi Tourism Authority (STA) – the national tourism organisation established in 2019 with a promise to welcome the world to Arabia. In this role, he is responsible for delivering the authority's mandate to build domestic and inbound visits by developing, packaging and distributing tourism offerings in collaboration with the industry. He also oversees the development of the Visit Saudi destination brand and the monitoring of visitor experiences.

Before taking on his current role, Fahd served as Chief of Investment, Strategy and Tourism Marketing for the Saudi Ministry of Tourism. In that capacity he played a leading role in launching the e-visa and introducing the Visit Saudi brand with a global campaign that established the kingdom as an exciting new tourism destination.

Formerly, Fahd was Chief Commercial Officer at King Abdullah Economic City (KAEC), where he led the destination management office and spearheaded marketing, corporate communications and sustainable development projects. Before joining KAEC, Fahd was Chief of Marketing and Competitiveness at the Saudi Arabian General Investment Authority (SAGIA), where he won five international awards for communications and advertising campaigns, and online marketing strategy.

In addition to sitting on the board of the Saudi Tourism Authority, Fahd is also a member of the board of trustees for the Prince Mohammad bin Salman College for Business and Entrepreneurship, the board of the Qiddiya Investment Company, the board of the General Authority for Conventions and Exhibitions and several government committees.

HTTPS://WWW.VISITSAUDI.COM

MALCOLM HENDRY

MANAGING DIRECTOR OF THE RUBENS AT THE PALACE HOTEL, HOTEL 41, BBAR AND 100 PRINCES STREET HOTEL

Malcolm Hendry has worked with Red Carnation Hotels for over twenty years, including the Chesterfield, Mayfair Hotel and the Milestone Hotel. In 2022 he took on the role of Managing Director for Hotel 41, The Rubens at the Palace, and Bbar, having previously been the general manager for all three properties over the last two decades. Malcolm is also Managing Director of 100 Princes Street, a luxury hotel in Edinburgh opened in 2023. Hotel 41 was voted the number one luxury hotel in the UK by Tripadvisor, The Rubens at the Palace is an iconic, historic five-star hotel and the Bbar is a restaurant and cocktail bar, neighbouring the two properties. 100 Princes Street is the first Scottish property for Red Carnation Hotels, and in his role as MD, Malcolm will bring the attention-to-detail and service level his London properties are known for to a new home in Scotland. Malcolm was voted the Top General Manager Worldwide in the Luxury Travel Advisor Awards of Excellence in 2019. This lifetime achievement award is undoubtedly one of many to come for a man who has personified hospitality and strong leadership throughout his career.

HTTPS://REDCARNATIONHOTELS.COM

DEMIAN HODARI

PROFESSOR OF CORPORATE STRATEGY AT
EHL HOSPITALITY BUSINESS SCHOOL, LAUSANNE

Consistently recognised as the best hospitality school in the world, École Hôtelière is located in Lausanne, Switzerland, where, for twenty-three years, Dr Hodari has spent his time teaching undergraduate and graduate-level students, as well as delivering executive education courses and facilitating strategic management workshops for hotel companies worldwide. Dr Hodari's research focuses on the strategic relationships between hotel general managers, owners and management companies, and has been recognised with awards from numerous organisations, including EHL where he was twice recognised as researcher of the year. In addition to his academic accolades, Dr Hodari speaks at industry events and leads strategy workshops and training seminars for hotel companies and their managers. To date he has trained over 3,500 industry executives. Prior to joining academia, Dr Hodari spent fifteen years working in the hotel industry, including as a hotel manager, consultant, president of an independent hotel management company and parking valet.

HTTPS://WWW.EHL.EDU

GEOFFREY KENT

FOUNDER AND CHAIRMAN OF ABERCROMBIE & KENT (A&K)

Geoffrey brings a truly extraordinary lifetime of experience, innovation and genuine passion to the world's most exclusive luxury adventure travel corporation. A pioneer of the modern luxury safari, Kent has taken his company, and his clients, from previously remote areas of the African continent to the furthermost reaches of the globe. In 1982 he founded the Friends of Conservation, of which HM King Charles III is the patron. It is a highly regarded, award-winning international organisation which seeks to preserve the endangered natural environment. Geoffrey Kent continues to travel the world in search of exotic destinations and has covered more than eighteen million miles to 156 countries. In between these expeditions and forays, he became a well-known polo player; he was captain of the A&K team in the US for more than twenty years and won the US Open twice, the US Gold Cup, the Cartier International and the most esteemed cup in polo, the Open Championship, the World Cup. Geoffrey Kent was a founding member of the World Travel & Tourism Council, the world's largest private-sector organisation dedicated to travel and tourism, serving as chairman for six years. In 2021 he was awarded the Global Icon Award and made an honorary member of WTTC. He was inducted into the UK Travel Hall of Fame for creating 'Experiential Travel' and was honoured by Travel Weekly with a Lifetime Achievement Award. He is a member of the United Nations Leadership Council for Sustainable Development Solutions Network.

HTTPS://WWW.ABERCROMBIEKENT.CO.UK

MARLOES KNIPPENBERG

CEO, KERTEN HOSPITALITY

Known as a pioneer of the modern mixed-use developments philosophy for lifestyle destinations that revolve around personalised experiences for all, Marloes's visionary leadership has helped carve an industry niche, where ESG rests at the core of operations, business processes, and the whole value chain of suppliers, owners, guests and teams. Amplifying the Kerten Hospitality brand from one brand in one country, seven years ago to a global lifestyle group with almost fifty projects, Marloes has always remained loyal to her mission. She seeks to continue expanding the lifestyle footprint across destinations where collaborations and a common purpose drive all stakeholders and builds longevity of projects by empowering local businesses and communities. Her journey in hospitality started with Hilton where Marloes held senior operational and commercial management positions for over a decade. But her greatest passion has consistently been nurturing young talent, advocating industry transformation and inspiring teams and peers to embrace a more sustainable agenda for people, communities and guests. As an avid supporter of a greener and more inclusive industry, she serves as an ambassador for the global Hospitality Student Challenge by Hotelschool, in the Hague.

HTTPS://KERTENHOSPITALITY.COM

RANI RAAD

(FORMER) PRESIDENT, CNN INTERNATIONAL COMMERCIAL

Rani worked at the global news network CNN International for a quarter of a century, including almost ten years as President. He was responsible for CNN's commercial functions outside the US and oversaw Turner International's programmatic trading. Previous to his role as President, Rani was Executive Vice President and Chief Commercial Officer of CNN International. He led the CNN International Commercial group since its creation in 2013, to align all international commercial activity into one organisation. Prior to that role, Rani was Senior Vice President and Managing Director for CNN International advertising sales. Rani began his career with CNN in New York and is now based in London. In 2013, he was listed seventy-one in the Arabian Business Power 500 list of the world's most influential Arabs, and in 2015 Rani was named by Arabian Business as the thirteenth most powerful Arab under forty. In 2011, the World Economic Forum recognised Rani as a Young Global Leader, for his contributions to the media industry. In 2015, Rani was named as one of Syracuse University's S.I. Newhouse School of Public Communications' 50 Forward – fifty alumni selected from Newhouse School's fifty-year history for their achievements in the media sector. Rani graduated with a B.S. from the S.I. Newhouse School of Public Communications at Syracuse University in New York.

HTTPS://EDITION.CNN.COM

CYRIL RANQUE

(FORMER) PRESIDENT, TRAVEL PARTNERS GROUP, EXPEDIA

Most recently President of the Travel Partners Group, Expedia for more than fifteen years, in this role Cyril was responsible for the integration of all travel partners through the marketing, distribution, data and technology solutions of the Expedia Group platform. Prior to joining Expedia Group, Cyril was Vice President of Marketing and Distribution for Louvre Hotels, having advised the Taittinger Group when the company was founded in early 2004. Previously, he was co-founder of Educastream.com, an online education start-up, head of the French CRM practice for AT Kearney, CRM consultant at Accenture, investment banker at Morgan Stanley in London and financial analyst at LVMH in Tokyo. Cyril is currently a board member of the Ritz Paris hotel and the European online travel agency Lastminute.com. He holds a master's degree from ESSEC Graduate School of Business in Paris, with a specialisation in finance and strategy, and currently lives with his wife in Geneva.

HTTPS://WWW.EXPEDIA.CO.UK

DAN RICHARDS

CEO, GLOBAL RESCUE COMPANIES

Serving as the CEO of Global Rescue since he founded the company in 2004, Dan is also the President of Crisis Services Company, a Vermont-based captive insurance company. He currently serves on the US travel and tourism advisory board at the US Department of Commerce, is a board member of Re:wild, a science-based environmental conservation organisation, is an ambassador for the US ski and snowboard team, and a global member of the World Travel and Tourism Council. Prior to founding Global Rescue, Dan spent a decade in the private equity and financial services industries. Over the last two decades, he has been involved in financing and private equity investments for more than thirty companies. Dan is a graduate of Middlebury College where he played football, rugby and was a competitive powerlifter. He received his MBA from the Tuck School of Business at Dartmouth College where he has served as an Entrepreneur-in-Residence.

HTTPS://WWW.GLOBALRESCUE.COM

JULIA SIMPSON

PRESIDENT & CEO, WTTC

Since 2021, Julia Simpson has been the President and CEO of the World Travel & Tourism Council, representing the private sector of the global travel industry. Founded in 1990, the WTTC is central to effective, equitable and sustainable advancement of the global travel ecosystem. Its founding mission endures – driving the growth of the sector in a way that ensures:

- governments recognise travel and tourism as a top priority
- businesses balance economics with people, culture and environment
- commitment to share the pursuit of long-term growth and prosperity

Prior to her role at WTTC, Julia spent fourteen years in the aviation sector on the board of British Airways and Iberia and as Chief of Staff at International Airlines Group. Previously, Julia was a senior advisor to the UK prime minister. She held a number of key positions in the UK government and in the public sector, including Director at the Home Office and the Department for Education and Employment; Assistant Chief Executive for the London Borough of Camden; and Head of Communications at the Communication Workers Union. Julia is on the board of the London Chamber of Commerce.

HTTPS://WTTC.ORG

GAVIN TOLLMAN

CEO, THE TRAVEL CORPORATION (TTC) GROUP

As CEO of TTC Tour Brands, Gavin Tollman leads the world-leading portfolio of tours for any and everyone, including Trafalgar, Insight Vacations, Luxury Gold, Costsaver and Brendan Vacations. For over three decades, Gavin has dedicated his career to revolutionising guided travel. In 2010, Gavin launched Trafalgar's exclusive 'Be My Guest' signature offering, pioneering the concept of local travel experiences enabling travellers to go beyond the guidebooks and meet locals in their homes, to break bread together, and to hear their stories. This idea demonstrated that travel can responsibly and sustainably assist the destination and not just the visitor. With a firm belief that travel should be a force for good, in 2010 Gavin also played a vital role in the launch of The Travel Corporation's not-for-profit, TreadRight Foundation. TTC's 'How We Tread Right' five-year strategy directly supports eleven of the seventeen United Nations global sustainable development goals. Gavin continues to challenge the status quo in everything he does, believing that travel can break down barriers, broaden horizons and enrich travellers' souls. Gavin was born into the hospitality industry in Johannesburg, South Africa and currently resides in Geneva, Switzerland.

HTTPS://TTC.COM

MATTHEW UPCHURCH

CEO, VIRTUOSO

A travel industry visionary with a lifetime of experience in numerous sectors, Matthew has led Virtuoso since its establishment in 1986. Today it consists of more than 20,000 of the world's most sought-after luxury travel advisors. As CEO of the industry's leading luxury travel network, Matthew oversees the company's marketing, sales, and operational systems with a focus on keeping the organisation ahead of the pack and the trends. He was the first recipient of the Luxury Travel Expo's 'Leaders in Luxury' award and was named among the 25 Most Influential Executives in the Travel Industry by Leisure Travel News. Matthew was named to the ASTA Hall of Fame in 2004 and the Cruise Lines International Association Hall of Fame in 2010 and has served as the chairman of the Travel Institute. In 2019, Matthew accepted the World Tourism Award, in 'recognition of Virtuoso's commitment to sustainable tourism practices; and its mission to make sustainability a greater factor in consumer choice when travelling to increase success for those who are dedicated to travel as a force for good'.

HTTPS://WWW.VIRTUOSO.COM

DARRELL WADE

CO-FOUNDER AND CHAIRMAN OF INTREPID

An Intrepid co-founder, Darrell was the company's CEO for more than twenty years and is now the group's chairman. From day one, he spearheaded Intrepid's journey to becoming a leader in sustainable experience-rich travel. A highly regarded entrepreneur and sustainability advocate, Darrell set up Intrepid in the late 1980s as a new way for people to explore the world that was immersive, sustainable and gave back to the communities they were visiting.

Darrell is vice chair of the World Travel and Tourism Council and chairs their sustainability committee. Darrell is chairman of Travalyst, the global partnership founded by The Duke of Sussex, that brings together Booking.com, Google, TripAdvisor, Expedia, Ctrip and Visa.

Darrell is also chairman of The Intrepid Foundation, the Dawn Wade foundation and social enterprise Good Cycles. Beyond travel, Darrell is active in the start-up and entrepreneurial ecosystems in Melbourne and beyond and is a co-founder and director of seed stage VC Skalata Ventures.

HTTPS://WWW.INTREPIDGROUP.TRAVEL

WILLIE WALSH

DIRECTOR GENERAL OF THE INTERNATIONAL
AIR TRANSPORT ASSOCIATION (IATA)

Willie is the eighth person to lead the International Air Transport Association (IATA) when he took on the role of Director General in April 2021. Prior to joining IATA, Willie had spent his entire career in the airline industry, beginning as a cadet pilot with Aer Lingus in 1979, rising to the position of Chief Executive at the airline in 2001. In 2005 he was appointed Chief Executive of British Airways (BA). He led BA through the 2008/09 global financial crisis, established a transatlantic joint business venture with Iberia, Finnair and American Airlines, and oversaw the 2011 merger of BA and Iberia under a newly established parent company, International Airlines Group (IAG). He was Chief Executive of IAG from its inception until September 2020. Under his leadership, IATA has focused on supporting the industry's emergence from the COVID-19 crisis as well as aviation's ambitious and historic commitment to achieve net zero carbon emissions by 2050. Willie has also strongly advocated for infrastructure partners to avoid recouping their COVID-19 losses from their customers including airlines and air travellers. A citizen of Ireland, Willie was born in Dublin, in 1961 and holds a master of science and business administration from Trinity College, Dublin.

HTTPS://WWW.IATA.ORG

HON. PREMIER ALAN WINDE

PREMIER OF THE PROVINCE OF THE WESTERN CAPE, SOUTH AFRICA

Prior to taking over the role of Provincial Premier, Hon. Premier Winde previously served in many of the province's ministries. His campaign for the premiership centred on improving education, healthcare, safety and public transport for the province. He has further committed to improving the efficiency of government service delivery through innovation and new technology. In 2009 he became the Minister of Finance, Economic Development and Tourism for the Western Cape. In 2014, he took up the position of Minister of Economic Opportunities, in charge of the Department of Agriculture and the Department of Economic Development and Tourism. In 2018, he became the Minister of Community Safety, and in 2019 he became the Premier-Elect of the Western Cape. Hon. Premier Winde enjoys spending time with his wife, Tracy, and children, Jason and Lauren. In his spare time, he is a keen cyclist and coffee drinker.

HTTPS://WWW.WESTERNCAPE.GOV.ZA

This book, this legacy project, is for each and every one of the leaders profiled and those around the world not yet profiled but who may want to be a part of this project as it evolves. To you we say, thank you.

EPILOGUE

*One of the greatest tragedies of COVID-19 is that it
didn't have to be this way. We have the tools and technologies
to prepare for pandemics better, detect them earlier, respond
to them faster, and communicate their impact.
But globally, a lack of coordination, a lack of equity,
and lack of solidarity meant that those tools were not used
as effectively as they could have been. We must promise
ourselves and our children and grandchildren that we will
never make those mistakes again.*

WORLD HEALTH ORGANIZATION (WHO) DIRECTOR-GENERAL
TEDROS ADHANOM GHEBREYESUS ON DECLARING AN END TO THE
COVID-19 GLOBAL HEALTH EMERGENCY, MAY 2023

As happens in life, and as time passes, memories fade. This is especially true when memories are about times of hardship, hurt and heartache: we make an effort to erase them, over-riding or over-writing them with new, happier ones. Life and lives move on, ultimately beyond our lifetime.

With the loss of memories, however, comes the loss of learnings that could protect us from times of hardship, hurt and heartache once more. So many of us have no understanding of the impact of global illness – how it can completely paralyse us as global communities, societies, possibilities. Polio, smallpox, the plague, the great flu – these were all major health crises once, but now they are very much relegated to history. Each crisis was in a different time, a different trauma, a different story. So too will be the case one day for COVID-19.

Today, as you read this, so much time has passed since those early days of the global pandemic. People have moved on. People have moved on to new jobs, new countries, new relationships, new interests, new opportunities. People are making new memories, memories to make up for those moments lost during almost three years of global disconnect, both physical and emotional. Time can indeed bring healing.

Time can also, however, bring betrayal. Time has the power to hide what is important for us to remember. It's incredible to think that there was a time, not that long ago, when we believed the ways in which we as humans connected, communicated, and cared were going to stop. There was this time when we thought that handshakes and business cards would no longer be a part of how we engaged in the business world. There was a time when we thought that blowing out candles on birthday cakes would stop as a way of celebrating each year that young and old were being loved and celebrated by those around them. There was a time when we thought offices would close, the need for communal spaces, communal working environments and meetings was eliminated as we could meet, workshop, attend conferences and network online. There was a time when we thought the sense of normal would never be what we once knew it to be.

And yet now we are living in a time where all of that seems fictitious. We are living in a time where it feels as if everything is simply normal in so many ways. We have been able to connect, communicate, and care the way we used to, relying on touch more than tech, relying on trust more than technical guidelines, relying on faith so that somehow we can move through even the hardest of storms, and indeed somehow we can see a faint rainbow on the horizon.

The signs are everywhere that another global crisis is starting to fade in our memories, but not this time. Too much has been gained alongside the losses. This period provides a mirror that allows us to look at how far we have come, how much strength we have gained, how much wisdom we have acquired, and how grateful we are for having made it through, together. For a very brief period of time there was an unusual intimacy in how people, including professionals, engaged with one another. Also, there was an honesty, and an emotional transparency, alongside a heightened level of trust and examples of exemplary leadership. As revealed through the pages of this book, leadership is not only about actions, but also about emotions, about intentions, and about attitudes to the future. This is one of the priceless legacies of the time we all shared.

The time spent writing this book has been one of intense analysis, examination, interrogation and also, blessing. Years from now when people pick up this book and read it, I deeply hope that they will gain an understanding of what happened, an appreciation for what it took to get us all through, alongside a respect for those who suffered unimaginable loss. In addition, this book will continue to offer people insight and inspiration as they face their futures. Whenever that time may be, wherever they may be, in that moment may they feel that they too can face whatever crisis is put before them, knowing that when they hear a calling they will be able to respond in a way that leaves them feeling proud for the decision that they made.

And so closes the epilogue to this book – the final word before one's manuscript goes to print, one's commitment to meaningful, helpful reading is put forward to a world of readers, one's story goes into literary history.

Thank you for being with me as a part of this time. x

A FINAL WORD OF THANKS

Writing this final section of *The Call to Leadership* is like going to purchase fresh flowers from a streetside florist on a sunny spring day – it makes my heart smile with such joy and it releases in my heart such immense gratitude.

It goes without saying that this book, this labour of love, would not have been possible without the honest, generous, unfiltered, unconditional support of the twenty leaders profiled. From the moment they accepted my invitation to be a part of this special project they turned each chapter into an honour. Each of them not only gave me their time, energy and attention, they also gave me their trust, their hearts and their deepest personal memories. For this I am eternally grateful . . . twenty times over.

As shared earlier in this book, the thesis of this project had the incredible blessing of examination by Dr Sanjay Gupta – one of the remarkable unsung heroes of the global pandemic and someone who heard the sincerity of my great 'ask'. Not only did he 'show up' for me, but he also reinforced my fundamental belief that whoever we are, whatever we do, however our lives have unfolded, we are all connected. We all bleed red. Sanjay, all the loving thanks in the world for the world of difference you make.

To the Secretary-General of the UNWTO, Zurab Pololikashvili, who kindly wrote the beautiful foreword to this book, thank you. Thank you, Sir, for being one of the first global leaders I witnessed in the early, early days of the pandemic who, with urgency and determination, reached out beyond the travel and tourism sector to mobilise leaders at the highest level in the WHO, ICAO, ILO, IMO, WTO and other vital UN bodies, as well as António Guterres, the Secretary-General of the UN himself. Importantly, not only did you express the need for solutions to be found to protect our global industry, but you fought to protect the global community as a whole.

A salute must also go to those who have so warmly given of themselves through the process of book development – personal and professional connections across the globe, and across stages of my life, who have been with me on this journey from concept to content, keeping me focused on not just what I was writing and how I was bringing it to life but why. These people include the late Jonathan Ball as well as Annie Olivier, Dr Julie Etellin, Dr Andrew Jennings OBE, Martin Towler, Johannes Zijlstra and Richard Bangs.

To the professional editing and publishing magicians who have taken my work and made it 'work' starting with the lovely Jess Lomas down under to the incredible team at whitefox right around the corner – John Bond, Julia Koppitz, Sarah Rouse and Kiana Palombo, thank you, exclamation mark in bold.

To Jack Ashley, Matt Brown and the team at ID Audio, thank you for guiding my words, thank you for guiding my voice. 'Thank you', with the volume turned up!

To Debbie Flynn and her team at FINN Partners, loving thanks for gently expanding my comfort zone to strongly magnify this book's message as needed to honour this time, and the lessons, that Mother Nature has given us.

To the official AM&A contributors in this book, Jessica Zijlstra and Grace Towler, my glass of bubbles is raised to them both with such loving thanks. Together they courageously, creatively, confidently, and when needed, compassionately, joined me on this journey from first brainstorming flipcharts to final image selections and manuscript edits. Together they rose to the incredible challenge of working through every word of my work and being honest in letting me know when something was not working. Together they form the invaluable easel on which I have been able to paint the canvas of this story.

Closer to home and closest to my heart:

To Sardarji who, through making me a 'Rotary daughter' from a young age, embedded in my DNA and heart the principle of 'service above self', and an ear to recognise the first sounds of a calling.

To Aidan, whose spirit has carried me through some of the hardest times since 'that moment' a lifetime ago when my wiring was firmly set and sense of purpose was made vividly clear.

And especially to Al Merschen who was bold enough to encourage me to start writing and keep writing and keep writing and keep writing when I heard this calling, brave enough to be one of the official manuscript reviewers, and kind enough to apply his expertise to launch this book in a way that would best promote and leverage this project yet stay true to me. He has also been unwavering in standing by me through every moment and milestone of our shared years, knowing what really matters to me and why.

Finally, and sincerely, to you reading this right here and right now. Thank you – thank you for opening your time, mind and heart to reading these pages, hearing these voices, and listening to your own within. I dearly hope that as you close this book you feel stronger for it. Throughout our lives we will all face many more challenges, individually and collectively, of that we can be sure. Whatever happens, whatever you may face, may this book leave in your heart trust in one core truth: you are not alone. x

ENDNOTES

1. https://wttc.org/about/about-us

2. Information from: Corporate Leadership Training Market Growth, Size, Trends, Analysis Report by Type, Application, Region and Segment Forecast 2022–2026 (June 2022) https://www.technavio.com/report/corporate-leadership-training-market-industry-analysis

3. www.jimcollins.com

4. Information from: Simon Balls, Global Distribution of a COVID-19 Vaccine: aviation's mission of the century? (December 2020) https://kennedyslaw.com/thought-leadership/article/global-distribution-of-a-covid-19-vaccine-aviations-mission-of-the-century/

5. Charlotte Seet, Emirates SkyCargo Has Now Transported 1 Billion COVID-19 Vaccines (April 2022) https://simpleflying.com/emirates-skycargo-1-bn-covid-19-vaccines/

RECOMMENDED READING

BOOKS:

Bessel van der Kolk, A., *The Body Keeps the Score: Brain, mind, and body in the healing of trauma.* (Penguin Group, 2014).

Bourla, A., *Moonshot: Inside Pfizer's nine-month race to make the impossible possible.* (HarperCollins, 2022).

Christakis, N. A., *Apollo's Arrow: The profound and enduring impact of Coronavirus on the way we live.* (Little Brown Spark, 2020).

Gupta, S., *World War C: Lessons from the COVID-19 Pandemic and how to prepare for the next one.* (Simon & Schuster, 2021).

Kennedy, J. F., *Profiles in Courage.* (HarperCollins, 1955).

Ripley, A., *The Unthinkable: Who survives when disaster strikes – and why.* (Crown, 2008).

Zelikow, P., *Lesson from the COVID War: An investigation report.* (PublicAffairs, 2023).

ARTICLES:

Crisis and Risk Emergency Communications: The psychology of a crisis. CDC (2019).

TRAVEL & TOURISM REPORTS/PUBLICATIONS:

To Recovery & Beyond: The future of travel & tourism in the wake of COVID-19. WTTC (2020).

Oxford Economics, *COVID-19 Analysis Fact Sheet. Aviation Benefits Beyond Borders.* (2021).

IATA Global Passenger Survey: 2021 Highlights. IATA (2021).

The Economic Contribution of Tourism and the Impact of COVID-19. UNWTO (2021).

McKinsey & Co. & IATA., *Understanding the Pandemic's Impact on the Aviation Value Chain.* McKinsey & Company (2022).

Effects of Novel Coronavirus (COVID-19) on Civil Aviation: Economic Impact Analysis. ICAO (2023).

A World in Motion: Shifting consumer travel trends in 2022 and beyond. WTTC (2023).

INDEX